y'all *twins?*

Kat & Margaret King

A delightful collection of short stories about real people and real events told in that Southern style spirit that is both appealing and a pleasure to read.

- Diane Z. Shore, Author
How to Drive Your Sister Crazy

Margaret and Kat have written a heart warming, yet funny, book of growing up in the South as told through the truthful eyes of innocent children. No matter where you grew up, you can certainly relate to their stories, because we all had similar experiences. Reading this book made me feel like I was sitting on the front porch at one of my own family reunions listening to my aunts and uncles tell stories of their own childhoods. Y'all Twins is one of the finest examples of true "Southern story tellin'."

- Ben Mitchell, Author,
Without One Plea

The charming story of the triumphs of twins Katherine and Margaret King will steal your heart. Certainly any member of that select group of the world of twins will relate, as will a generation of children of the '50s. The King twins' book is a joy to read. Their rich experiences growing up in Mississippi offer much wisdom for a wide audience.

- Michelle Leigh Smith,
Texas Writer

y'all *twins?*

Katherine and Margaret King

DeedsPublishing

Published by Deeds Publishing
Marietta, GA
www.deedspublishing.com

Printed in The United States of America

Library of Congress Cataloging-in-Publications Data is available upon request.

ISBN 978-1-937565-16-9

Books are available in quantity for promotional or premium use. For information, write Deeds Publishing, PO Box 682212, Marietta, GA 30068 or info@deedspublishing.com.

First Edition, 2012

10 9 8 7 6 5 4 3 2 1

ACKNOWLEDGEMENTS

First and foremost, we want to thank our editor, Luther Knight, author of four murder mystery novels. His words of encouragement motivated and pushed us to complete *Y'all Twins,* a series of stories from our childhood. Thank you, Luther!

We also send very special thanks to our first cousin, Dr. John King. He read every story, eagerly anticipating the next chapters before we could finish them. As it happened, he was the connection to getting *Y'all Twins* published.

We thank Deeds Publishing for their professionalism and confidence in us. The fact that they wanted us to succeed means the world to us, and we are so grateful for their help and support.

We could not have written this without our friends and classmates who grew up with us and helped create these memories.

We also want to thank our two proofreaders, Emilie Bramlett and Dicki King for giving our book their time and effort.

We also want to thank Linda Pope and Michael Goode for their creative contributions to *Y'all Twins.*

WE WOULD NOT HAVE SUCCEEDED WITHOUT EACH OF YOU!

DEDICATION

We dedicate this book to our family who helped form us into the people we have become. To our parents, Mary Cecile Dornbusch King and Travis Menton King; to our sister, Kirk and to our brothers, Bill and Allan; to our children, Elizabeth, Lee, Katherine, Carolyn and Taylor; to our grandchildren, nieces and nephews; to our sister-in-law, Nancy King and brother-in-law, Gene Bramlett; and especially to cousin Johnny.

TABLE OF CONTENTS

INTRODUCTION

There are a thousand small towns where thousands of souls just like us worried and wondered and grew up, despite all the roadblocks placed in the way. Our town, to us though, was different. Oxford was our little piece of the world, our haven, isolating us from the travails of the rest of Mississippi. Basically we loved this town because it made us feel secure in its warm closeness. Our sanctuary was a lazy, laid-back, indolent refuge. To us there has been some undefined sense of belonging to this intoxicating town that is compelling, as we have remained closely linked to it all of our lives.

Those were the years of innocence, the years of our childhood, coping with coming of age in rural Mississippi. These are our stories of the pains and joys and fears, told in a series of anecdotes, as we grew into adolescence.

We were born Katherine Cecile King and Margaret Elizabeth King on May 24, 1948, in Vicksburg, Mississippi. The oldest by twenty-five minutes, Katherine was quite naturally the dominant twin. The King family of five moved from Prentiss, Mississippi to settle into Oxford shortly after the twins celebrated their first birthday. Our brother, Bill, was eleven months older and the three of us were quite a handful. Three years later our sister, Kirk, arrived and three years after her birth our brother, Allan, was born. In a matter of seven years, there were five children, a large family by modern times.

The division of labor in our household was typical of the lifestyle that existed during the 1950s. Leaving before eight o'clock each weekday morning, Daddy entrusted all the daytime household duties and childcare to Mama. She had her hands full raising five children from eight to five each day. She was a strict, no-nonsense kind of Mama who expected to be obeyed. She took her job seriously and must have felt overwhelmed at times, but always in control of her young children. Much like the security of living in our small town, we felt the same reassurance in our family setting knowing that our parents cared deeply for us.

Our children requested that we write some stories from our childhood, stories that could be passed down to the next generation and those that followed. What started out as short stories of our antics soon escalated into a manuscript for publication. As we relived these tales, we wondered if other kids who were raised in our era may have experienced similar stories. Then we realized, probably not, because there were two of us and our childhood was quite unique. We are identical twins and that fact, in and of itself, was enough to set our childhood apart from others. We hope you enjoy reading our stories as much as we enjoyed remembering the tales and putting them into written form.

Y'ALL TWINS?

"Y'all twins?" That was the most frequently asked question of us throughout our childhood. Running a close second was, "Which is Which?" And you may be asking the same question as you look at the picture from our childhood on the front cover.

The pictures on the back cover, however, have a story to tell, and by the time you finish the book there will be little doubt as to, "Which is Which."

One special morning, waking earlier than usual for a school day "The King Twins" hopped out of bed eager to don their new identical outfits that had been carefully ironed and hung neatly in their closet. The finishing touches had been completed the day before when their Mama sewed the last of the buttons on both jackets. She had worked hard to get the two outfits sewn for this very special day. It was the day of the twins' first grade school pictures.

Dressing quickly in blouses and jumpers, the sisters laced their freshly polished saddle oxfords and raced pell-mell to the breakfast table. Once breakfast was over, the girls were directed to the bathroom where each took her turn sitting on the side of the tub. Their Mama meticulously parted each girl's hair and formed two perfect pigtails, one behind each ear.

She tied ribbons around each pigtail and gave strict instructions, "Don't you two mess up your hair at recess. I've fixed it just the way I want it for your school day pictures. Now, slip on your jackets and remember to take them off before you have your pictures made. I spent a lot of time sewing the blouses and jumpers, and I want them to show in the pictures. Do you understand me, Katherine? Margaret?"

"Yes, Ma'am," one twin replied as she looked her Mama in the eye, and the other twin nodded affirmatively as she fiddled with a hair ribbon.

When the school-day pictures arrived a month later, it was apparent that one twin had followed her Mama's instructions. And the other hadn't. So you decide, "Which is Which?

WHO IS HE?

On a late, sweltering afternoon in 1954, just after a summer shower, five gangly neighborhood kids between the ages of six and eight encircled the newly formed mud puddle. Sitting on the wet ground with legs splayed and dirty feet touching all around, our attention was focused on the freshly made mud pies stacked like hamburger patties down at the local snack shack during the noontime rush.

Clapping my hands together to remove the excess dirt, I instructed, "Everyone get just one pie and take it to be cooked." Turning to our best friend, I continued, "Rita, you go first. Margaret and I made a stove behind you over there. See?"

Pointing in the direction of the make-shift oven, Margaret jumped up ahead of Rita and raced to place her pie on top of the bricks, followed closely by the rest of the gang. While the pies baked as the sun beat down on them, we all returned to the circle to create more.

Invoking seniority over us, our eight-year-old neighbor, Carol, sought to persuade us to take a bite of one of the unbaked pies.

"Here," she said. "This is good for you. And it tastes so good, too."

We responded as one, "Yuck, no way!"

I chimed in, "If it's so good, then you eat it first. I'm gonna tell Mama that you're tryin' to make us eat this stuff."

With my threat hanging over her, Carol bolted for her house next door and slammed the screen door behind her. At that moment a familiar sound echoing down the street caught our attention.

"Come on y'all," our older brother Bill yelled. "Hurry, he'll be here real soon. Hear the clompin'?"

Scrambling to our feet, Bill, Rita, Margaret, and I raced to the thick hydrangea bush at the front corner of our house. There we scrunched low to hide from the familiar figure coming toward us from the far end of the street. Like spies, we pressed the leaves aside to get a better glimpse of the approaching one-man parade.

A barely audible whisper escaped Bill's lips, "Y'all be quiet. Wait like we always do 'til he passes the house. Then we make a run for it. He's not goin' very fast today so we can catch it easy."

"Hold on tight and don't let go 'til we get to the end of the street," I added conspiratorially. "Then jump off and run like crazy for home."

"I don't wanna go today. I still gotta splinter in my little finger from yesterday. See?" Margaret whined as she thrust her pinkie finger for each of us to inspect. "I don't wanna go," she repeated.

"Well, you're goin' if we go," Bill insisted. "And we're goin' when I count to three. Ready, get set, one, two, three, go!"

All four, mud splattered, barefoot and naked as jaybirds to the waist, sprinted for the back of the mule-drawn buckboard. We climbed on and sat quietly with our backs to the driver, hoping he had not noticed his extra passengers. A light breeze blowing from up the street cooled our sweaty skin. We giggled, delighted by this joy ride to the corner of our street. Thrilled at having stolen a ride, Bill laid back looking up at the clouds, relaxed and carefree. But white knuckled, we girls clinched the back end of the buggy swinging our legs freely to and fro, while wiggling muddy toes.

The smell of the mule made its way to the rear of the wagon as the wind kicked up slightly. "Pee-yew, that mule stinks doesn't it?" Margaret muttered while fanning her hands back and forth in front of her face to dissipate the foul odor.

Bill sat up abruptly and signaled that it was about time to jump off. Signing with his fingers, one, two, three, he jumped and was followed quickly by the rest of us. Slowing down to make a right turn, had our chauffeur glanced over his right shoulder, he would have seen eight dirty feet fleeing back up the street.

Laughing, I shouted for all to hear, "Last one home is a rotten egg."

All four dashed away from the buggy, retracing the path to our house. Margaret panted, tears welling up in her eyes, "Stop! I'm outta breath! My side's hurtin'! I can't breathe! Don't leave me! Stop! Wait for me! What if he comes back to get me?"

Stopping to wait for Margaret to catch up with us, we turned only to see a bobbing finger pointing in our direction, a warning gesture from the man in the carriage. He knew.

"Wow, that was close. That scared the dickens outta me. Maybe we shouldn't do that anymore," Margaret said between gasps.

"Aw, that wasn't so scary. I thought it was kinda fun. Quit bein' a big sissy," I scolded my twin sister.

"Yeah, let's do it again tomorrow," Bill said enthusiastically, then looking at each of us added, "Want to?"

"Why not? It's fun jumpin' on the back of that ol' wagon and ridin' to the end of the street. Let's do it just one more time, okay?" I pleaded.

The following day, Saturday, was full of outdoor chores with Daddy directing. As the end of the day approached, Daddy was push-mowing the front yard. Margaret, Bill and I took turns sweeping the driveway and hauling pruned branches away from the house and yard. The all too familiar sound of the approaching mule-drawn buggy stopped us dead in our tracks. We ran for the safety of the front steps as Daddy waved to the pipe-smoking man sitting on the buggy's wooden bench behind the flop-eared mule. Stopping to chat with Daddy, the driver pinned us with a stare as we huddled uneasily on the concrete stoop. Smoke escaped from the pipe while he returned his attention to the conversation, with an occasional glance in our direction. Momentarily, he took a white handkerchief from his britches and wiped his brow before cramming it back into the pocket. We sat frozen and mute as only garbled words met our ears. Daddy mouthed, "Bill, Katherine, and Margaret," and pointed us out.

Tipping his hat to the three of us as a goodbye gesture and with the slightest grin, the thin-faced man nodded before turning to pick up the reins and continue his daily route.

As the buggy continued slowly down the street, Daddy strode toward us and asked, "Do y'all see him often?"

With our heads bowed and peering up at Daddy, Bill answered for all, "Yes, Sir. Who is he?"

Daddy replied, "He lives down the street and around the corner. Says he sees y'all playing out here all the time. Is that true?"

Jerking my head up to reply quickly, "Uh-huh. Yes, Sir. He rides by here a lot with that pipe in his mouth. And it makes the air smell so good. But when that ol' mule goes to the bathroom, it really stinks. Who is he, Daddy?"

"He's our neighbor. You three stay away from his buggy and don't bother him. You understand?"

Margaret chimed in, "Yes Sir, Daddy. We won't bother him again. I promise. What's his name, Daddy?"

"Mr. Faulkner. Mr. William Faulkner," Daddy said softly.

MY NAME IS BILL

"Come on y'all. Here comes Mr. What's His Name," Kat shouted excitedly as she ran for the familiar hiding place behind the hydrangea bush.

"His name is Mr. Faulkner," our older brother, Bill, said for the hundredth time.

"Yeah, that's who I mean. Him. He's comin' with his ol' mule. Come on, let's watch him."

Kat, Bill, and I scrunched behind the flowering bush, peeked through the leaves to see the pipe-smoking man ride toward us in his mule-drawn buckboard. We never grew tired of spying on him, especially since Daddy told us weeks ago to not ever bother him. As he approached, he slowed and glanced in our direction.

"You think he can see us?" Kat whispered.

"Don't know. But he's lookin' straight at us, isn't he?" I whispered back.

"Shhhh," Bill admonished. "Y'all be quiet. He can't see us but if y'all keep talkin', he'll hear us."

Worried that the man would see us and report to Daddy that we were spying on him, we scrunched even lower, prisoners in our own front yard.

Picking up the reins, the overall-clad man turned his attention back to the task of directing his mule down the street.

"Whew," I said. "Don't think he saw us or heard us, do y'all?"

"Naw. Reckon why he slowed down when he got to our house?" Bill asked almost to himself. "It seemed like he was lookin' for us. Wonder why?"

"I think he misses us ridin' on the back of his buggy to the end of the street," Kat responded.

"Yeah," I chimed in. "Maybe he's lookin' for us and wantin' us to ride with him."

"Naw. Betcha he's lookin' for Daddy," Bill said as he ran to the curb to watch the retreating buggy. "He's slowin' down and lookin' back at us."

Not knowing what else to do, we waved at him, a friendly gesture on our part.

"Look! He's turnin' around and comin' back," I said nervously.

"Let's run and hide. Come on y'all, let's get outta here," Kat said anxious to escape.

"Don't run," Bill shouted. "He's holdin' up his hand. I think he wants to talk to us."

"Do you think he knows we've been spyin' on him?" Kat asked.

"Don't know, but I think we should stay 'til he gets here," Bill replied.

We sat on the curb awaiting the return of the mule and buggy, each hoping we were not in trouble, but fearing that we were.

"Y'all Travis King's children?" the strange man asked as he pinned each one of us with a stare.

"Yes, Sir," we responded as one, jumping to our feet to get a better look at the man and his mule.

Looking ill at ease, Kat suddenly blurted, "Does that ol' mule poop everywhere?"

With a slight trace of a grin, the thin-faced man ignored Kat's question and pointed to the two of us. "You two are twins. What are your names?"

"Her name's Margaret and mine's Katherine. And this is our brother, Bill. We're not botherin' you are we?"

"Well, Bill, my name is Bill," he said turning his attention to our brother.

"Sir, my real name's William," our brother informed the stranger.

"And my name is also William," the man offered.

Confused, Kat turned to look at our brother Bill and asked, "Well, which is it? Is your name Bill or William? I didn't know your name was William." She looked up at the man who called himself Bill and William and continued, "So you are Mr. Bill William? My brother's name is Bill, not William."

"Our Mamas named us William," he said pointing to Bill and himself. "Our friends call us Bill."

"Yes, Sir," Kat responded, still a little confused. Changing the subject, she continued, "Okay, Mr. Bill, we're not botherin' you are we? My Daddy told us not to bother you anymore. We're sorry, aren't we?" Kat turned toward us, hoping Bill and I would add apologies as well.

I stayed mute, but Bill smiled and spoke up, "Yes, we're sorry we ever bothered you. We won't do it again."

Then everyone's attention was focused on me so I blurted out, "Don't tell Daddy we bothered you today. He told us not to and we hafta mind him. So don't tell on us, please."

Appearing to be deep in thought and after a long draw on the pipe, Mr. Bill appeared to be on fire as the smoke expelled from his mouth and nose enveloped him.

Amazed at the swirling smoke, Kat exclaimed, "That's a good trick. Can you do it again? That pipe smoke smells good."

I elbowed Kat in the ribs, hoping she'd stop talking just as a response came in answer to my plea, "Don't worry, Margaret. You are Margaret, aren't you?" he asked.

"Yes, Sir," I answered shyly, not meeting his gaze.

"I guess you think I told on you the Saturday I stopped by to talk to your Daddy. I had a question to ask him about the cedar trees in my front yard. When I saw the three of you sitting on the porch, I wanted to know your names. That's when your Daddy pointed you out to me. That's all we talked about."

"You mean you didn't tell him 'bout the times we hitched a ride on the back of your wagon?" Kat asked.

"I didn't think it necessary. But you could get hurt doing that and I don't want to see you get hurt. So when I drive by, just wave at me and I'll wave back. Deal?"

"That's a deal, Mr. Bill, uh, Mr. William, uh, what's your last name?" Kat blurted out.

"It's Mr. William Faulkner. Can't you remember that's what Daddy told us? But his name is Bill, isn't that right?" brother Bill asked proudly as he stared into the gaunt face.

He tipped his hat at us, picked up the reins and "clicked" the mule into action.

"Bye, Mr. Bill William Faulkner!" Kat yelled as the back of his hand signaled his goodbye.

We sat down on the sidewalk together amazed at the encounter with the man on the wagon. Not giving up on a good time, Kat mused, "Don't 'cha think we can ride on the back of that ol' wagon just one more time?"

KICKIN' AND SCREAMIN'

A few days before Labor Day 1954, while we gathered for breakfast, Mama made light conversation, "I have something important to tell you girls." Dividing her attention equally between us, she continued, "School days are right around the corner, and you'll be starting the first grade. You are big girls now, and you are going to have to act like big girls. Can y'all do that for me?"

"Oh yes, Ma'am. What do you want us to do?" I asked aching to please her.

Mama didn't answer, but addressed my sister instead, "Margaret, you can be a big girl, too, can't you?"

Margaret's eyes gleamed with excitement. Expecting a wonderful surprise and liking the way the conversation was going, she answered enthusiastically, "Yes, Ma'am. I'm a real big girl."

Daddy joined the conversation, saying, "Margaret, come sit on my lap and let me talk to you about what your Mama and I are getting at."

"Can I sit on your lap too, Daddy?" I asked feeling left out.

"Of course you can, Katherine. Come over here and let me talk to both of you," he said in a gentle voice. He scooted his chair from the table to make room for us. "Hop up here."

We jumped onto his lap, one on each leg. He gave us a kiss and cleared his throat saying, "The three of us are going to run an errand downtown this morning. And, if you're good girls, when we're finished we'll end up at the Kream Kup for some ice cream. How does that sound?"

Bill and Kirk stopped eating, now interested in the conversation taking place. Each chimed in, "Can I go, too? I want some ice cream."

I glared at them, addressing their outbursts, "Daddy's talkin' to us, not you. He wants to take me and Margaret to the Kream Kup, not y'all. Isn't that right, Daddy?"

"Yes, today I'm taking the twins. I'll take you another time," Daddy answered, looking directly at Bill and Kirk.

"Anyway," Margaret said staring at Kirk, "You're too little to help Daddy run his... What did you say it was, Daddy? Errats?"

"That's right, an errand," Daddy said, hugging Margaret close to him.

Turning our attention to Daddy's earlier question, we squealed and giggled with delight as we blurted out, "Can we have chocolate ice cream?"

"You can have chocolate ice cream if you are extra good girls," Daddy said.

"We'll be good won't we, Margaret?" I knew it was going to be a great day for both of us.

"Yeah. But can't we get the ice cream first? We'll be extra good if you let us get the chocolate ice cream first. Can we, Daddy? Can we?"

"Well, I don't think so. I need to talk with you about where we'll be going before we get the ice cream," Daddy said, reluctant to discuss what began to sound like a delicate subject.

I started to respond, but something deep in my mind popped up. *Why did Daddy seem different?* "Okay, Daddy, where are we goin' first?" I inquired, just a little apprehensive. "The post office or the grocery store? We'll be happy to go with you anywhere you wanna go."

"Well," Daddy said hesitating, "We need to go to the Square and tend to some business."

"Okay, Daddy. That'll be fun. We'll be good while you do your benness," Margaret said.

"Well, it's not exactly *my* business I'm taking care of," he said, carefully weighing his words. "You see, we're going to the health department this morning to get your shots. Each of you will be getting three vaccinations."

Eavesdropping, Bill blurted, "They gonna get the ones that hurt real bad? You know, the ones I got last year?" He continued, eyes twinkling, "It hurts for days, and that needle is as long as a pencil. It hurts so bad you think your arm's gonna drop off."

"That's enough from you, Bill. No need to scare the twins any further," Mama admonished.

"No!" Margaret screamed, slamming her fist on the table before she bolted from Daddy's lap. "I'm not gonna get shots," she shouted over her shoulder as she scrambled, half falling, up the stairs to her room and locked the door.

I followed closely behind. Panicked to find the door locked I beat on it, begging, "It's just me. Let me in before they come and get me. I'm not gonna go without you. Come on please, Margaret, open the door so we can hide from 'em."

She cracked the door just wide enough for to me squeeze through, then grabbed my arm, and dragged me in, all the while watching the stairs for possible pursuers. Once I was inside, she slammed the door behind us, locking it again.

Margaret ran to the window and called, "Come here and help me open the window. We can jump out and get away. Hurry. They'll be comin' for us soon," Margaret chattered in a panic.

"Are you crazy? We can't jump outta that window!"

Stopped by the thunderous rap on the door and the rattling of the knob, we froze in our tracks, wide-eyed and scared nearly to death.

Daddy's firm but gentle voice broke the silence, "Girls, unlock this door. I just want to talk to you."

"No, Daddy, I don't wanna get shots," Margaret wailed like a maniac.

Outside the door we heard Bill say, "Here, Daddy, use this to unlock the door. I use this hair pin all the time. It's my secret weapon when I wanna get in their room. Want me to open it for you?"

"Go ahead, son, open it," Daddy directed. There was a hint of resignation in his voice.

Before they could open the door, Margaret and I scrambled for hiding places. I ran into the closet while she slid under the bunk bed.

"I'll find 'em, Daddy. Want me to find 'em for you?" Bill asked excitedly as he rushed into the room ahead of Daddy.

"No, Bill, I'll take it from here. You go back downstairs and help your Mama with the dishes," Daddy instructed.

"But I know where they are. Please let me find 'em for you," Bill begged.

"No. I'll find them myself. You can leave now and shut the door behind you," Daddy said firmly.

A dejected Bill backtracked.

I heard the bed creak as Daddy's weight settled onto it.

"All right, you two, come out from your hiding places and talk to me." Daddy's patience was growing thin.

We didn't budge, afraid to move. Trying desperately not to breathe lest we be found, we remained quiet as little mice.

"Don't forget, we're going to get ice cream afterward. Maybe even a milkshake," he bribed, softening his voice a bit.

That got to me. "Really, a milkshake?" I poked my head out of the closet, forgetting I was supposed to be hiding. "Did you hear that, Margaret, a chocolate milkshake. That's okay with me, Daddy." I proudly pointed out to him, "She's under the bed. Come out from under the bed, Margaret. Daddy's gonna get us a chocolate milkshake. Don't 'cha wanna chocolate milkshake?" I rambled on as I peeked at her hiding under the bed.

"No!" came her firm reply. "You can't make me go. I'll stay here the rest of my life. You can't make me go!" she squealed.

"Here she is, Daddy. I can almost reach her. Come down here at the end of the bed and we can pull her out," I shouted for him to help.

"I'll get her myself, Katherine. Let me handle this."

"No, leave me alone. I don't want any ice cream or a milkshake. Just leave me alone," Margaret screamed through sobs.

Daddy's long arms reached for her legs. From the foot of the bed he tried gently pulling her free while Margaret kicked and screamed bloody murder. She held onto the bed springs with all her might, but finally Daddy's strength won out. All the time I was leaning over the foot of the bed watching Margaret's feet appear, followed by the remainder of her small-framed body.

"It's okay, Margaret. We're gettin' a milkshake after 'while. It won't hurt too awful bad, will it, Daddy?" I inquired hesitantly.

"It will only hurt for a few minutes and then it will be all over," Daddy said, trying to console the frightened little girl. He picked her up and held her in his arms, trying to comfort her and calm her nerves.

Sobbing and gasping for breath, Margaret clung to Daddy as if it would be the last time she would ever see him. He then picked me up with his free arm and carried us down the stairs. He put us in a chair in the living room, directing us to stay seated.

"I'm going to start the car, then I'll be back to get you," Daddy said firmly.

Once Daddy had left, Bill ran into the room and, enjoying our misery, announced, "Remember Rita had her shots last week and they hurt real bad."

Margaret began screaming and crying again. I jumped from the chair and ran toward Bill with both fists flying. He bolted from the room with me on his shirttail. Realizing that he had stirred a hornet's nest, he raced to the kitchen where Mama was washing dishes. Using her as a human shield, he stuck his tongue out, knowing he was home free.

"I'll get you later," I mouthed to him, shaking my left fist. Before Mama could intervene, I retreated quickly to the chair where Margaret was sitting and resumed my place beside her. I patted her on the leg trying to comfort her, "Just remember we're gonna get some ice cream and if we're extra good, maybe a milkshake. And it'll be fun to bring it home and slurp it in front of Bill," I said doing my best to convince her, but not being all that confident myself.

The front door opened and Daddy walked in saying, "Let's go, girls."

That brought on a new bout of screams and kicks from Margaret. Daddy bent down and scooped us up, one on each arm, and walked through the front door.

Margaret was fighting him all the way to the car, screaming, "No! No! Don't make me go!"

"Where y'all goin'?" our closest friend and next door neighbor, Rita, asked. She continued, "I was hopin' y'all could come over and play with me this mornin'."

"We'll play when we come back from gettin' our shots. And after Daddy gets us our milkshakes," I yelled to her from the car window.

"I'm glad I'm not gettin' any more shots. They hurt like crazy. Remember those shots I got last week? Look, my arm is still red and puffy. And it's still achin' pretty bad," Rita commented innocently as the car rolled out of the driveway.

Still crying, Margaret let out a loud shrieking sound, "I don't wanna go get any shots. I don't wanna. Daddy, don't make me go."

I was getting pretty irritated at Margaret's behavior. She was going to cost us a great treat if she didn't stop hollering.

"Be quiet. Daddy is gonna get mad at us and then we won't get any milkshakes," I whispered repeatedly during the short drive to the health department.

Her rampage continued all the way to just off the northeast side of the Oxford Square. Daddy parked the car in front of the health department clinic, got out and opened the back door. As it swung open, Margaret scrambled to the opposite door where I was sitting, just out of Daddy's reach. In her effort to escape, she climbed over me and reached for the door handle. Having my fill of her tantrums I pushed her back across the seat, hard. Daddy grabbed her and tried to pull her from the car. Margaret locked her feet under the driver's seat and was holding onto the door handle with all her might. I came to Daddy's rescue and pried her fingers from the handle. As Daddy lifted her from the car, she again began kicking at me wildly.

His hands full with Margaret's kicking and screaming, Daddy shouted, "I can't pick you up, Katherine. Follow beside us and open the door for me when we get there."

So I acted like a big girl and walked beside them up the sidewalk to the health department, excited that I would get a treat, but doubtful that Margaret would.

"Okay, Daddy. Do you think I can get a chocolate milkshake? I've been really good. Margaret has been bad but I haven't."

Daddy didn't seem to hear me. He yelled, "Open that door and let's get this over with!"

Once inside the door, the antiseptic smell caught me off guard. I started crying, associating the awful smell with the impending shots. With both of us crying uncontrollably, Daddy handed us over to the nurse. She must have had experience doing this as she held Margaret in a tight grip with one arm and clutched my wrist with her other hand. She turned to escort us into the shot dungeon.

"Mrs. Keel, do you need my help back there holding the girls down?" Daddy asked, raising his voice to be heard over our screaming.

With so much caterwauling we only heard the words, 'kill' and 'holding the girls down.'

"Don't let her kill us, Daddy!" I yelled.

"The nurse's name is Mrs. Keel," he explained. Of course, we couldn't hear.

"You're gonna kill us!" Margaret screamed as she writhed in Mrs. Keel's embrace.

"She's not going to kill you," Daddy raised his voice, more than a bit irritated at us. Looking at the nurse he shouted, "I'll hold each girl still while you shoot them."

That comment restarted our wailing. "Don't shoot us. Please don't shoot and kill us," I screamed, as I squirmed to get loose from Mrs. Keel's grasp.

Two nurses rushed to aide Mrs. Keel. One of them, a tall, lanky one, grabbed Margaret and disappeared with her down the hall.

The other nurse, a grey-haired lady picked me up, hauled me to a separate room, pointed her finger at me and commanded, "Sit in that chair by the window and don't get up. Do you hear me?"

I managed to snuffle in a quavering voice, "Yes'um."

I could hear Margaret down the hall screaming, "Let me go! Daddy, where are you?! Daddy, come get me! Save me, Daddy! I don't wanna die!"

The nurse started talking to me, trying to calm me down but I paid her no attention. I was worried about my sister somewhere down the hall. Reality hit when the nurse wiped my arm with a cotton swab. It was cold and wet and smelled putrid. Just then I saw the second nurse hold a needle up vertically and squirt something out of it as she came toward me. I bolted from the chair and headed for the door, only to find it locked. When I turned back around the first nurse grabbed me and pinned my arms to my body as the needle sank into my arm. I let out a blood-curdling scream and began kicking at both nurses. Once the needle was extracted, the nurse holding me loosened her grip slightly. I took this opportunity to free myself from her, to escape her clutches. Once out of her grip, I ran in circles around the room dodging the determined nurses.

Finally, out of frustration, the first nurse poked her head out the door and hollered, "Mr. King, we need your help."

Daddy entered and in two strides captured me. Once he picked me up I had no wiggle room. The nurse gave me the remaining vaccines in quick order. I screamed bloody murder and thought I was about to die. But to my surprise, I didn't. It was all over and I survived. My arm hurt like crazy, but I survived.

Once the ordeal was over, Mrs. Keel asked, "Would you like a sucker?"

"Yes, Ma'am," I replied. "Where is Margaret? I hear her cryin'. Where is she?"

Mrs. Keel replied a little more kindly, "She's down the hall and that's where we're headed. Mr. King, will you come help us?"

Daddy put me down and followed the nurses down the hall to wrestle with Margaret.

I also followed and stood outside the door listening to her screaming, "Don't touch me. Daddy, please help me. Save me, Daddy. No! Get that needle away from me!"

She screamed with all her might as the needle plunged into her arm. Once Margaret received all the vaccines, the ordeal was finally over and she bolted from the room where all the action had taken place. She saw me, grabbed my hand and we ran through the lobby, out the front door. We jumped into the green, four-door family sedan and cowered in the back seat, weeping silently. Our arms were already throbbing, as predicted by Rita and Bill earlier that morning.

When Daddy joined us in the car, I whimpered, "Can we go get some chocolate milkshakes now?"

"Do you girls think you deserve a treat?" Daddy asked, knowing the answer.

"Oh, yes, Sir," Margaret said trying to control her crying. "I think we did real good," she said in a quivering voice.

"Yes, Sir, Daddy. We did *real* good. Don't 'cha think we did?" I implored.

He looked at us and with the slightest grin, turned, cranked the car and headed to the Kream Kup.

We arrived home with ice cream cones in hand and showed off these rewards to an envious Bill.

"We were real good so Daddy took us to the Kream Kup and bought us chocolate ice cream cones," I rubbed it in.

"I thought y'all were gonna get chocolate milkshakes," Bill commented trying not to show too much envy.

"We were good, but Margaret acted up on the way to get shots, so he wouldn't get us milkshakes, just ice cream," I explained.

Mama saw our tear-streaked faces and, knowing the answer, still asked, "How did it go, Travis?"

Daddy just rolled his eyes and shook his head. He finally answered, "I've had better days. They both went kickin' and screamin'."

Later that day, during lunch as we gathered around the table, Bill asked, "Is your arm hurtin'? Why are you holdin' it down by your side like a soldier, Margaret? Is it 'cause it's sore?"

"Yes, Margaret. If you'll move your arm, it won't hurt so much," Daddy advised her.

"Yes, Sir, Daddy. But it hurts so much to move it," Margaret replied, holding her sore left arm with her right hand and forming a pained look on her face.

"Why don't you take my hand and squeeze it," Daddy said as he offered his right hand to Margaret.

She slowly raised her arm to the table and reached for Daddy's hand and held it tight for the remainder of the meal.

I looked to my right to see if maybe Mama would hold my hand. She gave no indication of wanting to do so, but smiled and patted my shoulder before returning her focus to the tomato sandwich she was eating.

Oh well, I thought, a little envious of Margaret's tender moment with Daddy, as I took a bite of the peanut butter and jelly sandwich.

MIRROR IMAGES

The week before school started in 1954, Daddy arrived home at the usual time of 5:15 P.M. Margaret and I rushed to be the first to jump into his arms as he closed the car door. We welcomed him home with a great big hug and a kiss on each cheek.

Mama had supper cooked and was dishing out portions on plates. As soon as Daddy washed up, he came into the kitchen and joined the family at the table.

Looking at Margaret and then at me, Mama said, "Now that you've had your shots I want to tell you that when you start the first grade next week, you will be in separate classrooms."

I returned her gaze, curious as to what that meant. Faltering, I finally asked, "What do you mean? We'll be in two classrooms?"

"Well," she began, "you will have different teachers. Margaret will be in Mrs. Leeper's room and you," pointing a finger in my direction, "will be in Mrs. Blassingame's room."

"Mrs. Who?" I asked, puzzled. Then I continued, "What did you say her name is?"

Mama answered, enunciating, "Mrs. Blass N Game."

"Why can't we be in the same room?" Margaret whined.

Entering the conversation, Bill added, "Margaret, you'll love Mrs. Leeper. Her room was close to my room last year and I could hear her sometimes teachin' kids to read and write." Of course he had to add, "And she'll paddle you if you're not good."

"I'll be good," Margaret said, glaring hard at Bill.

"But I don't understand why we can't stay together," I groused.

"Your Daddy and I think you will do better if you are not together all the time," Mama explained.

Her reason seemed lame to me, but before I could complain, Margaret broke in, pleading, "Oh, but we *love* bein' together. We don't wanna be apart. Can we stay together, *please?*"

"I know this will be your first time in school, but your father and I think having you in different rooms will be better for both of you. So we are going to try separate classes this year to see how y'all do," Mama said, leaving no doubt she was in no mood to argue with us.

We knew there was no point in trying to plead our case, so we shrugged and suffered quietly through the remainder of the meal.

That night, when we crawled onto our bunk beds, neither of us knew what to say. Finally, I leaned over from the top bunk, looked down at Margaret and whispered, "I don't wanna be in another room from you."

"Yeah," Margaret said looking up at me with maybe the hint of a big tear welling up. "It makes me sad. It won't be any fun without you in my room. Do you think we can beg 'em into lettin' us be in the same first grade room?" she continued, sniffling.

"I don't know. Sounds like they've been talkin' about it for a long time. But we can always meet up at recess and play together. There are some big swings on the playground, and I can push you and then you can push me. We'll have fun seein' how high we can swing. I hope we have sweet teachers. What's the name of your teacher?" I asked.

"Mrs. Leeper. Remember, Bill said she's nice. But I don't know who your teacher is. What did Mama say her name was? I forgot already," Margaret said.

"Mrs. Bisseling. Or somethin' like that. I never heard that name before. Have you?"

"Naw. It was somethin' funny like that. I hope you'll like her. Anyway, it makes me feel sad 'cause I won't be in there with you," Margaret teared up.

"It'll be okay. Don't cry. We'll always be best friends, huh?" I asked with a lump in my throat.

"Wanna come down and sleep in my bed again? Just don't hurt my arm 'cause it's still real sore from those shots we got last week," she suggested and started to move over to make room for me.

"Okay. Sure," I said as I jumped from the top bunk, landing lightly on the floor. "You don't hafta move, I'll just crawl over you to the other side of the bed. I won't hurt you."

We fell asleep that night as we had done almost every night of our lives, comforted by the nearness of each other.

The week following Labor Day, our family of seven piled into the green sedan shortly after 7:30 in the morning to take the short trip to the elementary school one block west of the square. Margaret and I were excited and scared at the same time.

"Y'all hafta be good in school or you'll get a paddlin'," Bill reminded us, smirking.

"Don't worry 'bout us. We'll be good," Margaret said excitedly, refusing to be baited by Bill. "I hope Rita will be in my class." She turned toward Daddy and said, "I'm scared, Daddy." Before he could respond she continued, "I'll be extra good today 'cause I don't wanna get a whippin' the first day of school."

Then not to be outdone by Margaret, I said, "I'm scared, too." When he didn't acknowledge I added, "Are y'all gonna leave us there all day?"

Mama had been silent until now, but at my question she explained, "You'll be there part of the day and I'll pick you up after school. When you get used to first grade, I'll let you three walk to school and home afterward. But for now, your teachers will look after you until I pick you up."

Daddy parked the car on the Square, a full block from the school. Bill jumped out of the car as soon as it stopped moving and ran to sit on the front steps of the schoolhouse.

"Daddy, will you hold our hands?" I implored. "Mama's holdin' Allan and has Kirk's hand, so will you hold ours? We're scared 'cause we won't be together all day," I added, looking up at him.

Daddy took each one of us by the hand and walked us up the steps of the school where Bill waited. We climbed the stairs to the second floor and dropped him off in Mrs. Duncan's second grade room.

"Maybe I'll see y'all at recess after 'while," Bill said as he waved goodbye.

The next stop was to drop Margaret off. The six of us entered Mrs. Leeper's classroom. She looked at me, then at Margaret, then back at me, before addressing Mama and Daddy, amazed, "These girls are identical. How am I ever going to know which one belongs in my class? They are adorable and just alike. I declare, they are just alike."

We looked up at Daddy as he responded, "Well, their personalities are different. You'll just have to get to know Margaret and then you'll know them apart. It'll be easy. I'm sure you'll be able to tell them apart in no time."

"Okay. Which is Which? Which one of you is Margaret?" Mrs. Leeper asked.

I looked at Margaret and she looked at me as Daddy pointed to me and said, "This is Katherine here on my right." Patting my sister on her head, Daddy continued, "And this is Margaret."

"Okay," Mrs. Leeper said bending over and getting eye level with us. "How am I ever going to tell you two apart? You're dressed exactly alike right down to the red bows around your pigtails."

"Yes, Ma'am. Mama makes two of everything we wear. But we're different. But not much," I said turning my attention to the desks perfectly aligned in six rows. I turned back to Mrs. Leeper and asked, "Where's Margaret gonna sit? Which one of these desks is hers?"

"Well, I'll put everyone in alphabetical order and then she'll know where to sit," Mrs. Leeper explained patiently.

"What's 'betical order?" I asked, wondering what that big word meant.

"It's by the alphabet—A B C order. Your last name begins with a K, so I'll put your sister in line behind J," Mrs. Leeper clarified.

"Okay," I said, shrugging my shoulders at Margaret. Then turning back to Mrs. Leeper, "So, does that mean she will be in the front or the back of the room?" I asked trying to get a fix on where my sister would be placed.

As I looked around the room wondering where Margaret might sit, a small boy walked up to us and said shyly, "Hi. My name's Bill Bryant. My mama says y'all are twins. Is that so?"

Before either of us could answer, a small crowd of children and grownups were gathering around us looking curious. Some lady bent over us and staring directly into our faces, asked, "Y'all twins?"

"Yes, Ma'am. We are," enjoying the attention we were getting.

"Well, Which is Which?" the lady asked.

"I'm Katherine and she's Margaret," I answered directly.

"Oh, their names don't rhyme," she announced to the crowd, then turning back to us asked, "Why don't your names rhyme? I thought all twins had names that rhymed."

I looked at Margaret and shrugged, not knowing what to say, then looked at Mama for help in answering the lady's question.

Before Mama could answer, the lady pressed on, "You know, like Jan and Ann, Bill and Will. Like that."

Mama rescued us, interrupting, "That's enough for now, girls. It's time we get Katherine to her classroom. Come, let's go," she continued as she leaned over and gave Margaret a tight hug.

As we left, I turned at the door to say goodbye. Margaret was looking at me tearfully. I ran back to hug her and whispered, "It'll be okay. I'll see you at recess. Mrs. Leeper, when is recess?"

"Well, let's see. I believe it's at 10:15," Mrs. Leeper replied.

I looked up at her, brows furrowed and asked, "Is that a long time from now?"

"Oh, my, no. It's just a few hours away," she said smiling down at me.

"Mrs. Leeper says I'll see you real soon," I said to reassure Margaret, who had not said a word since entering Mrs. Leeper's room.

Another final hug, I left holding Daddy's hand again as we walked purposefully down the hall to catch up with Mama, Kirk and Allan.

The closer we got to my classroom a strange odor wafted my way. "Daddy, it stinks down here. Wonder what that smell is?" I complained.

"That's the cafeteria," he said pointing out the big room to the right. "It's where you will eat lunch each day. They'll cook you some good food and you can have chocolate milk every day. You'll like that, won't you?" Daddy countered.

"Chocolate milk will be good. Hope we don't have peas and carrots. Maybe we'll have peanut butter and jelly sandwiches or fried chicken. That would be good," I mused.

Mama held out her hand to stop us a few steps past the cafeteria. "Here we are at Mrs. Blassingame's room. Let's go in."

I walked in and gushed, somewhat awed. "This is a lot bigger than Margaret's room. Is that my teacher way down there in the red dress? Look at that mirror over there. It's so big. Will you pick me up so I can see myself in it? Maybe I can sit on the back row close to this mirror."

"Let's go meet Mrs. Blassingame and she'll show you where your desk is," Daddy said, hoping to distract me.

We strolled to the front of the classroom and waited in line to meet Mrs. Blassingame. I let my eyes wander around to become familiar with my surroundings. There were red birds, blue birds, and yellow birds pasted to the wall in different sections of the classroom. Desks were in rows just like in Mrs. Leeper's room. Bold printed A B Cs and numbers were posted above the chalkboard behind Mrs. Blassingame's desk. To the left there was a solid wall of windows allowing bright light to filter through. Outside, magnificent magnolia trees stood tall. I silently hoped I'd get a chance to climb them. My attention turned to the back of the classroom and refocused on the wall-to-wall mirror.

Standing beside me was a sandy-haired little girl tightly clinging to her Mama's hand. I mumbled more to myself than to the little girl, "Wonder what that mirror is in here for? My sister's room doesn't have a mirror."

I turned to the little girl and saw she was staring wide-eyed at me. "You have a sister?" she asked.

"Yeah, my twin sister's in Mrs. Leeper's room. I'm Katherine. Her name's Margaret. What's your name?"

"Deborah Carol. Deborah Carol Slade. But you can just call me Debbie. Everybody but my Mama calls me Debbie. She calls me Debrorah Carol. Am I gonna to get to meet your twin sister? I've never met twins before. Do you look just the same?"

"Guess so. Everybody says we do," I responded to the curious little girl. "Everyone is always wantin' to know Which is Which. So, do you know why that mirror's in here?" I asked her, anxious to have that question answered.

"My mama says it's for teachers who are still students but I don't know what that means, do you?" Debbie answered with her own question.

Before we could finish the conversation, Mama turned me around and nudged me forward announcing, "Katherine, meet your teacher, Mrs. Blassingame."

"Hello, I'm Katherine," I said shyly.

"Katherine, I'm Mrs. Blassingame. I understand you have a twin sister. Do you two look alike?" she queried.

"Yes, Ma'am. People say we do. But I can tell us apart," I rambled, realizing that was a dumb thing to say.

Smiling at my attempt to make conversation, Mrs. Blassingame pointed to the middle row, third desk back and directed me to take my place.

Mama and Daddy walked me to the assigned desk, kissed my forehead and whispered, "Bye, see you after school. Be good."

"Okay, Mama. I'll be good," I promised and really I did mean it.

I sat there waiting for the minutes to tick by until time for recess. When the bell rang, Mrs. Blassingame lined us up to go outside. I saw Margaret in the hall, and we ran outside, hand in hand, to the merry-go-round.

"I've got somethin' in my classroom that you don't have," I boasted.

"What is it? An animal or fish tank?" she questioned, her eyes sparkling.

"No, it's a great big mirror. I met a little bitty girl with a grown-up name, Deborah Carol Slade, and she said it's for students and teachers or somethin' like that," I replied.

"That's kinda funny, isn't it? I wanna see it when we go back inside," Margaret responded. "Rita's not in my class, was she in your room?" she asked changing the subject.

"Nope, she's not in my room. You wanna go sit in my class so you can see the mirror and I'll go sit in yours?" I asked, getting back to the subject at hand. "My desk is in the middle row and the third desk back. Where do you sit?"

"Third row, front desk," Margaret replied.

"You're on the front row? Wow! Don't think I'd like that," I blurted out. "We'll meet up at lunch and switch back, okay? Look for Deborah Carol Slade but call her Debbie. She likes to be called Debbie. She's really little and has a pink bow in her hair," I shouted as we each ran for the lines forming at the back door of the school.

I moved slowly in line to Mrs. Leeper's classroom. Third row, first desk was easy to find. I sat down and looked up to see Mrs. Leeper holding some crayons. When all of us were seated, she glanced around the classroom to see if we were all present. Next she passed out pictures of birds, and I spent the time before lunch coloring them blue. When the bell rang to go to lunch, I eased out of Margaret's seat and lined up for the restroom before marching single file to the cafeteria. Mrs. Blassingame's class was already seated at lunch tables, so I joined Margaret after getting a tray of food and grabbing the chocolate milk from the end of the assembly line.

I whispered, "Did you see the mirror?"

"Yeah, wonder why it's so high up. I had to jump up to even see my face. Wonder why that is?" Margaret asked.

"Don't know why a mirror would be so high. It goes to the ceilin'," I recalled.

"And only grownups can see themselves in it. And there's only one grownup in my room," I responded, a bit confused.

"We gotta ask Bill 'bout this. Do you think he'll know what's goin' on?" Margaret inquired as she pushed peas and carrots around her plate. "What kinda meat is this? Looks like it might be meatloaf, but I'm not gonna try it. Are you?"

"Naw. I'm not gonna eat it, but the roll is good. You gonna eat your roll?" I asked hoping she would hand it over to me.

"Yeah, it's real good," she said and took a bite.

"I colored a bluebird before lunch. What did you do?" I asked.

"They started learnin' the ABCs, but I already know 'em. Guess I'll go back to my class since I've seen that ol' mirror," Margaret said and then noisily slurped the last bit of chocolate milk from the carton.

Before I could respond, we were being herded back into a line to return to the classrooms. We looked around to see our classmates taking their trays to a hole in the wall and leaving them there. So we followed behind them, then hurriedly took our places in line.

Upon returning to my classroom, Mrs. Blassingame informed us that we would be taking a nap. Before I drifted off to sleep, I pondered the mystery of the mirror.

After the short nap and a lesson in arithmetic, the second recess bell rang. Margaret and I ran as fast as we could for the swings. We took turns pushing each other to the highest limits.

"Mrs. Leeper told us that school will be over as soon as we get back from recess," Margaret offered.

"That's great. I can't wait to talk to Bill when school is over. Think he'll know anything 'bout that mirror?"

"I don't know 'bout that. But look, everyone's runnin' back to the buildin'. Recess must be over. Come on, let's hurry or we'll be late," Margaret said nervously.

I lined up for water. By the time I got back to my classroom, school was over for the day. Following Mama's instructions, the three of us met her on the sidewalk in front of the school and made our way home.

Playing in the sand box before supper, I asked Bill, "Have you ever seen that big mirror in Mrs. Blassingame's room?"

"Yeah, they call it a two-way mirror. You can see what's goin' on in your classroom from the other side of the mirror," Bill explained.

"Really?" I questioned, weighing his every word. I thought about what he said for a moment then added, "Well, I gotta see it for myself. I don't believe it. There's no such thing as a mirror that's two ways."

"Is, too. Just go in the room next to your classroom and you'll see what I'm talkin' about," Bill chAllanged.

The next morning when I got to my classroom, I inspected the mirror firsthand by scooting a chair in front of it. Climbing onto the seat and cupping my hands to my eyes, I peered into the mirror. Nothing. It was just a mirror, plain and simple.

At lunch, Margaret and I made plans to skip the second recess to check out the mirror from the room next door. We agreed to meet in the restroom, and when the coast was clear, sneak into the adjacent room like Bill suggested.

When the second recess bell rang we walked swiftly to the restroom, glancing over our shoulders to see if one of the teachers was watching. Once inside the restroom we waited for a minute or so and then peeked out to make sure the coast was clear. No one was in sight so we stepped into the hall and walked to the door next to my classroom. Hesitating before entering, we looked at each other then opened the door. To our surprise it looked like a living room with a sofa, chairs and tables. I hurriedly pushed a chair over to the wall that joined my classroom and looked into it. I could see Mrs. Blassingame at her desk.

"It *is* a two-way mirror, Margaret!" I exclaimed, a little too loudly. "Come here and look. I can see my teacher. Oops, she's goin' into the little room behind her desk. Come look."

"Wow, Bill was right," Margaret admitted after joining me on the chair.

"Hurry, get down and go to my room and let me see if I can see you," I urged.

"Okay. I'll wave at you," she responded.

Margaret stepped into the classroom and I could see her all right. She began waving wildly at me and jumping up and down. Mrs. Blassingame heard the disturbance and came out of her office to investigate.

Confused at Margaret's wild antics, she blurted, "Katherine, what are you doing in here jumping around like that? It's recess. Don't you know you should be outside?"

"Yes, Ma'am, I know. I've been wonderin' about this mirror and wanted to see if I could see myself in it so I was jumpin' up and down tryin' to see myself," Margaret stammered.

I could see everything going on and decided it was time to make my escape, but had to rescue Margaret first.

I opened the lounge door, pressed my back to the wall and crept quietly to the doorway of my classroom.

I overheard Mrs. Blassingame tell Margaret, "Katherine, you have broken the rules. This is just the second day of school and you have deliberately disobeyed me." Pointing to the opposite corner of the back wall, she continued, "I want you to stand in the corner until recess is over. I'm going back to my office and I don't want you to move. Do you understand me?"

"Yes, Ma'am, but…," Margaret tried explaining before being interrupted.

"No *buts* about it, young lady. You'll stand in that corner and think about what you've done," Mrs. Blassingame said, continuing to point to the back wall.

I watched my teacher walk to her office and when the coast was clear, I ran to rescue Margaret, saying, "Run as fast as you can. Go outside 'til the bell rings. I'll stand in the corner. I'll be okay. Hurry, before she comes back in here."

Once recess was over and school was out for the day, Margaret came looking for me. She stood in the doorway, eyes lowered, hoping I would hurry up. Mrs. Blassingame dismissed all the students but me.

She called me to her desk, looked up and saw Margaret standing in the doorway.

Surprised by Margaret's presence, Mrs. Blassingame instructed, "Come in and let me see you two together."

I jumped in explaining, "This is my twin sister, Margaret."

"Yes, I can see that, Katherine," Mrs. Blassingame chuckled.

I'm sorry I was bad at recess. Please don't tell Mama and Daddy. I promise I won't ever be bad again," I begged.

"I'm going to hold you to that promise, Katherine. Now the two of you can go," Mrs. Blassingame directed after inspecting us closely.

"Yes, Ma'am," we said, as we took each other's hand and skipped down the aisle and out the door.

Once outside the door I whispered to Margaret, "Did you hear what she said when we were leavin'?"

"Naw, but I did hear her say my name. What did she say?" Margaret asked.

"She said, 'If I didn't know any better, I would have thought it was Margaret standing in the corner. No, it couldn't have been.'"

"Wow. That was close. Let's get outta here," Margaret said, checking over her shoulder to see if Mrs. Blassingame was following.

Exchanging conspiratorial grins, we dashed to the safety of the sidewalk to wait for Mama.

THE FOX STOLE

After Sunday school the second Sunday in November of 1956, Mama and Daddy gathered all five of us from our classes and collectively moved up the hall to the sanctuary of the Methodist Church. Standing in the center of a semi-circle and facing us, Mama voiced last-minute reminders on proper conduct in church, warning us, "I expect each of you to sit still, *no* touching each other and *no* whispering. Do you understand me, Allan? Kirk? Bill? Margaret? Katherine?" She eyed each of us as she asked the question, but focused most of her attention on me.

"Yes, Ma'am," came the reply in unison from all five.

As we walked past the pulpit to the pew, Mama did her best to separate Margaret, Bill, and me so that we weren't sitting next to each other. Margaret and I tried to manipulate the seating order by hanging back, as neither of us wanted to sit by either adult. On this particular Sunday, Allan entered the pew first, followed by Daddy, Kirk, Mama, Bill, Margaret, and me. I slumped onto the bench, happy to be on the end and as far away from Mama and Daddy as I could get. I turned around and noticed we were only about ten rows from the back of the church and wished I could escape outside into the crisp fall air. Coming toward me was an old lady with a purple tinge to her hair. I elbowed Margaret to get her attention but she just elbowed me back, glaring at me to stop.

Elbowing her again I whispered, "Look at that lady comin' toward us. She's got purple hair and looks like she's tryin' to cover it up with that hat. And it looks like she's tryin' to cover up her face with that fish net. You think she's tryin' to hide that purple hair?"

"Yeah. Wonder how she got purple hair?" Margaret chirped in, keeping her voice low.

Instead of turning into our aisle, the old woman settled into the pew in front of us. She sat down directly in front of Margaret and me, giving us the opportunity to take a closer look at the brown, bowl-like hat that featured a petite red rose perched on the side. The hat's mesh veil covered her eyes and nose. Margaret stared at her multi-colored hair of purple, blue, gray and white, all mixed up together as it dangled from beneath the hat.

"*What's that?*" Margaret mouthed, pointing at the woman's shoulders.

I followed her gaze to the old lady's back and gasped at the sight of an animal perched atop her shoulders. I lurched backward and grabbed Margaret's arm, almost ready to climb over the back of our pew.

Bill watched our reactions to the animal and quickly whispered to Margaret, "It's a dead fox, but it really looks alive, doesn't it. Tell Kat it's dead."

"I heard him. I heard him say, 'It's dead,'" I told Margaret as we relaxed, let out a deep sigh of a relief, and leaned toward the critter to get a better look. "Ask Bill what she's doin' with a dead fox around her neck. Is she off her rocker or what? And look, it's bitin' its tail. Yuck!" I said, disgusted.

I could hear Bill's answer as clearly as if he were talking in my ear. "I betcha she found it dead on the side of the road one day, took it home and stuffed it."

Shocked at this bit of news, I peered at the varmint from the left, then the right. It, in turn, stared back at me with its beady eyes. It glared at me no matter my viewpoint. We watched in awe as she removed the tail from the fox's mouth and then from around her neck and placed it carefully across the back of the pew. We scooted backward, drawing up our legs and feet so that we were sitting on them. We were frightened at the toothy grin that was permanently plastered on the fox's face. We were now eye-level with it. Wide-eyed, we glared at the creature then at each other. Margaret elbowed Bill and the three of us began to snicker. We were on a roll, but trying to stifle uncontrollable laughter. We knew this was *not* the time or place to be giggling since we were supposed to be on our best behavior. And if we kept it up, we would be in big trouble. The longer we stared at the fox head, the more we shook with laughter. I finally turned my back to Margaret and tried to find something as a distraction. I opened my purse and began counting jacks. But I was still shaking with laughter. Finally I turned my attention back to the fox. It was still glaring at me.

Our antics didn't go unnoticed by Mama. She leaned into Bill, placed her arm across his legs and shook her pointing index finger as a warning gesture to the three of us. We got her message and momentarily stifled our giggles.

I fidgeted around until I could stand it no longer and very quietly whispered to Margaret, "Touch it."

"No! You touch it. Are you sure it's dead? It's not movin'. Bill said it's dead. Do you believe him?" came her barely audible reply.

"I don't know, but I'm gonna touch it."

"Better not. You'll get in trouble," she warned.

Suddenly loud organ music sounded and we turned our attention back to the church service. The congregation rose in unison to begin singing a hymn. We quickly followed suit, placed our open purses on the floor at our feet, grabbed a hymnal and opened it to a random page. The purple-haired lady lifted the fox off the back of the pew and gingerly placed it around her shoulders, reconnecting the head and tail. I resisted the urge to reach out and touch the nose which was less than a foot away. We were now eyeball to eyeball with the animal. Staring at it intently, we noticed it had reddish brown fur, a pointed nose, ears pinned back and these beady black eyes. The small animal seemed to be grinning at us with sharp gleaming teeth and a permanent look of surprise plastered on its face. As if she knew we were staring at it, the gray-haired lady shifted the fox from her left shoulder to atop her right one, directly facing Bill.

He reached out to touch it, but had second thoughts when Mama gave him a stern look, shaking her head, whispering, "No."

All three of us were totally mesmerized by the dead animal as it glared at us and we glared right back. We had never seen a real fox before, alive or dead. Here one sat on the old woman's shoulder, right in front of us! We were not interested in singing, so we took this opportunity to whisper back and forth with each other.

I whispered to Margaret, "Ask Bill if the teeth and eyeballs are real. The eyeballs could be fake you know. They look like marbles."

"Are the eyeballs real?" I could hear her ask Bill.

Bill slowly moved his head up and down confirming that the eyes were indeed the real thing. With the hymn coming to an end, we began giggling again and knew we had to stop the laughter before the song ended or we would be in serious trouble.

Once the song was over, we sat and I nudged Margaret, "I'm still gonna touch it. Next time we get up to sing I'm gonna touch that ol' fox's head."

"No. You better not," Margaret whispered louder than she should have. "You're gonna get in lots of trouble."

Mama's head turned our way. In an effort to keep us quiet, she reached her arm around Bill's back and tapped Margaret on the shoulder. Margaret, in turn, nudged me, We skittishly turned our eyes to Mama, who put an index finger to her lips, a warning signal to behave.

Ignoring Mama's warning, I mouthed, "Don't worry, I won't get caught. I just *gotta* touch it."

Within minutes we were rising to recite The Apostle's Creed. Once again the old lady dropped the fox on the back of the pew within arm's reach.

I opened the hymnal and handed it to Margaret, ordering, "Cover me."

She strategically placed the hymnal between the fox and Mama, hiding my hand from view. I reached out to touch the dead animal. It was as soft as the stuffed animals on my bed. I petted it until we sat down to listen to the sermon.

The fifteen minute sermon was long enough for me to work up my nerve to touch the eyeballs; first I wanted Margaret to feel how soft the fur was.

I leaned over to her and whispered, "You gotta touch it. Feels like your stuffed dog. Really, it does. Touch it next time we get up. I'm gonna touch the eyeballs. I gotta touch the eyeballs to see if they feel like marbles."

Margaret shook her head no, gesturing to me not to touch it again. But I didn't pay her any attention, determined to put a finger on both eyeballs. The opportunity came during the last hymn.

We rose and I repeated my order to Margaret, "Cover me again."

We glanced to see that Mama was turned toward Allan, which gave us the perfect opportunity to touch the fox's eyeballs. Once again Margaret lowered the hymnal into place. I rubbed my fingers all around both eyeballs. I was amazed at how much they felt like cold glass. They could have been marbles.

I turned to Margaret, begging, "Come on, touch the fur, then touch the eyes. They're cold and feel like marbles. Go on, touch 'em before the song ends. Don't be a scaredy cat!"

Taking the chAllange, Margaret patted the fur. Moments before the song ended I grabbed her hand and jabbed her fingers into the eyes of the fox. Suddenly one eyeball rolled out of the socket and disappeared. Shocked, we looked at each other, wide-eyed.

"It fell out. The eyeball fell out. Look what you did!" I exclaimed in a tense whisper. "Where did it go? We gotta find it and stick it back in that eye hole."

"It's not my fault! You made me do it. It's your fault," Margaret hissed between clinched teeth.

"Never mind 'bout that. We gotta find it fast. Where could it be?"

Bill overheard the whispering and pointed toward the floor. He used his unlaced shoe as an excuse to lean over and search for the missing eyeball.

"It's not down there. Bet it rolled under her feet," pointing to the owner of the fox. "Y'all are really in big trouble now," Bill announced. The joyous singing covered our voices.

"Not me. I told her not to play with the eyes and she wouldn't listen," Margaret said, almost matter-of-factly.

"Better not tell on us," I warned in my most intimidating voice. "We'll find it. I'm sure we will."

But as church ended we were in shock because none of us could locate the missing eyeball. We stared, dumbfounded, at the one-eyed fox. We couldn't believe what had happened!

I nudged Margaret and whispered, "Looks like it needs an eye patch to cover up the eye hole. We better get outta here before that old lady notices it's gone."

Mama and Daddy were busy helping Allan and Kirk get their fall coats on. Luckily, Mama was so focused on our two-year-old brother that she had not observed any of our shenanigans.

Meanwhile, Margaret and I grabbed our purses and took this opportunity to escape the church. Once outside, I was desperate for Margaret to come up with a believable answer. "What do you think happened to that fox eye?"

"Don't have a clue," she responded. "Guess it rolled down the aisle. Wanna go back in and try to find it?"

"No. Do you think Bill will tell on us?" I asked, worried that Mama and Daddy would find out what we had done. "He loves to rat us out, you know."

"Don't think so. He was misbehavin' about as much as we were. Let's go find him and make sure he keeps his trap shut," Margaret said.

Confronting Bill as he walked out of the church, Margaret pressed him to remain silent, "Better not tell on us or we'll tell on you. I didn't mean to pick that eye out. I touched it and it just fell out. It was an accident. Please don't tell Mama and Daddy."

"I know you didn't mean to do it but you shouldn't been pickin' at that fox stole," Bill responded as if he had never misbehaved.

"Fox stole. What do you mean fox stole? I thought you said she picked that dead fox off the street. Now you say she stole it. So which is it?" I demanded.

"Yeah, you didn't say it was stolen. Why would she steal that ol' dead fox anyway?" Margaret added.

Bill explained, "It's a stole but it's not stolen. They are two different things."

Margaret interrupted asking, "Is it or isn't it stolen?"

"As I was sayin', it's a fur stole. That's what it's called. A fur stole. It wasn't stolen. She bought a stuffed fox. That's all I know. Now, let's figure out what we're gonna do," Bill continued. Our secret seemed to be safe with him.

"Yeah, what's that old lady gonna do when she finds out the eyeball is missin'?" I asked.

"Don't know. Let's get outta here before she comes out!" Margaret was anxious to leave.

We ran for the car, piled into the back seat, and shut the door as quickly as possible. Nothing was said on the way home about our behavior in church. We hoped Mama had not seen what we had done. Once Daddy parked the car, we bolted for our rooms and waited for lunch to be served, *dreading* the time at the table. We feared the topic of our misbehavior would be the only conversation.

As Mama handed Bill his plate of food, he looked up and innocently asked, "Mama, will you explain to Kat and Margaret what a fox stole is? They think it's been stolen."

Before we could rebut Bill's statement, Mama turned her attention to us and quizzed, "Why do you want to know about that?"

I shrugged my shoulders, leaving Margaret to answer the question.

Bill jumped in explaining, "We saw one at church today on an old lady's shoulders."

Hoping to change the subject, I added, "Yeah, Mama, why did that old lady have purple hair? Why was her hair purple and blue?"

Before answering, Mama turned to pick up another plate of food. As she handed it to me, she explained, "Well, she had purple hair because she dyed it that color."

"Yeah, and the fox is dead, too," Kirk added.

"Not that kind of dye. The fox was dead, yes. But the lady's hair had a hair color put on it and that is called, d-y-e, instead of d-i-e, which is what the fox had done – died," Mama continued.

"Did you see that fox stole, Mama?" Bill asked, steering the conversation back to where he wanted it to go. Was our secret safe with Bill, who was ever the teaser?

I gave Bill a swift kick under the table, a stern look and showed him a knuckle sandwich, which I hoped would shut him up. But it didn't.

On a roll, Bill continued, "That was a pretty red fox. I wonder why she wanted to wear a dead fox around? Don't you wonder, Kat?"

Suspicious at the conversation, Mama asked, "Is there something I need to know about that fox stole?"

"Oh, no, Ma'am, it's just pretty, that's all," Bill said with a grin as big as the one on the dead fox.

Declining desserts for the first time ever, we asked to be excused.

"You may be excused, but when I call you to come help with cleaning the kitchen, I want you here pronto. Margaret, you can dry the dishes. Katherine breaks too many of them. She can sweep the floor," Mama said.

"Yes, Ma'am," we both said as one.

We pushed past Daddy's chair, deposited our dishes in the sink and skipped to the back of the house, hoping nothing else would be said about that ol' fox.

In our room, I sighed, "Whew, that was close. I'll get back at Bill. At least we know Mama didn't see us pick the eye out of the socket or know that it's missin'."

"Yeah, I know." Margaret whined, "What are we gonna do?"

"I really feel bad about that fox's eye. I know that lady is wonderin' what happened to it. Wish you hadn't touched it," I said as I reached for my purse, adding, "Wanna play jacks?"

"You made me do it... sure... can I go first? I bet she can't wear it anymore 'cause it only has one eyeball." Margaret was not so quickly distracted from the present dilemma. "What's she gonna do with a dead fox with only one eye? Why does anyone want to wear a dead animal that bites its tail anyway?"

"Yeah, it looked real funny with only one eyeball," I said. I started to giggle about it all over again.

"We couldn't stop laughin' at it in church, could we? We almost got in lots of trouble, huh? Reckon where that eyeball is? I'd like to find it and give it back to her. I feel real bad 'bout it, you know?"

"Yeah," Margaret said thoughtful. "Let's play jacks and try not to think 'bout it anymore."

"Okay. They're in my purse," I said, as I dumped the contents onto the floor.

"Do you see what I see?!" Margaret asked as the jacks and marbles rolled out.

"How did *that* get into my purse?" I asked, glaring as the fox's eyeball rolled toward Margaret. "Pick it up and give it to me."

"I'm not touchin' that thing," she said with determination.

"It's not gonna bite you. It's just like a marble. Now, quit bein' a sissy and hand it to me," I demanded, adding, "Can't believe I was just wishin' I could find it and give it back to her. And here it is, big as you please!" I said, leaning over to grab it. "Let's see if it's a good shooter. Gather up my marbles and let's play."

Margaret shouted, "No, I'm not gonna play marbles with that ol' thing. We gotta figure out how to get it back to that old lady. You got any ideas?"

"Naw, I can't think of anything. I can't believe it was in my purse all this time. I guess that ol' eyeball fell out of that fox's head and landed right in my purse. We just gotta figure out what to do with it."

Margaret suggested, "Well, I betcha she'll be in church next Sunday and you could give it back to her then."

"You're the one who knocked it out so you gotta be the one who gives it back to her," I insisted. "I'm just tryin' to help you figure out how to do it." I had conveniently forgotten who had jabbed Margaret's fingers at the fox's eyes. I tossed the eyeball up in the air, catching it like a small ball, then pitched it to Margaret. "Catch it."

She jumped out of the way as the eyeball landed on the floor by her foot.

I snatched it back, saying, "I think this must be a *real* eyeball. It's too small to be a marble. And it doesn't roll around like a marble does."

"Stop playin' with that thing," Margaret scolded. "We need to figure out how to return it to that old lady."

"Okay, but we'll have to figure out what to say to her. What do you think we outta tell her?"

"I don't know. Just tell her you found an eyeball in your purse, and you think it belongs to her fox," Margaret answered.

"Hmmmm," I pondered. "Not sure how I'm gonna go 'bout tellin' that old lady that I found her dead fox's eyeball in my purse."

"Oh, I forgot, Mama said we're going back to church this afternoon for some home-made ice cream. Maybe the old lady will be there and you can give it back to her," Margaret said excitedly.

"Yeah, that's a good idea. Now, let's play some jacks. I'll let you go first. Here, catch," I said, as I threw the ball toward her.

Later that afternoon at the church ice cream social, we stood in line hoping there would be enough ice cream for us, all the while keeping an eye out for that old lady.

Bill ran up behind us, whispering excitedly, "That old lady with the purple hair, you know the one with the fox stole that has only one eye? That old lady is just comin' through the door. See, there she is now. You better go hide." Bill, who always seemed to enjoy trouble when it was Margaret's and mine, was delighted to egg things on.

"No, didn't we tell you? That ol' eyeball fell into Kat's purse. We found it. We're gonna give it back to her," Margaret gloated.

"I'm gonna go with you when you give it back to her," Bill butted in.

"Oh, no you aren't. Leave us alone so we can think what to tell her," I retorted.

"Are you 'bout to give it to her?" Bill asked.

"Yeah, as soon as we finish our ice cream, Margaret's gonna give it back to her," I explained.

"No, *I'm* not gonna give it back. *We're* gonna give it back *together,*" Margaret insisted.

"Okay, okay, we're gonna give it back together. Now quit whinin'." Turning to Bill, I continued, "Now, get lost."

We watched the old lady's movements as we ate our ice cream, waiting for the perfect moment to present the eyeball to her. She settled into a chair at a table that was unoccupied.

I elbowed Margaret, saying, "She's sittin' by herself. Let's give it to her now."

"I betcha she's waitin' on the long line to shorten. Why don't we take her some ice cream?" Margaret suggested, proud to have come up with such a perfect solution.

We walked together side by side, purses hanging casually from our arms and stopped at the table where she sat. "Would you like some ice cream? That line is too long to stand in and wait for some," I said, pointing over my shoulder. "Here, we brought you this." I thrust a bowl of ice cream under her nose and insisted, "It sure does taste good. It's vanilla. I think you're gonna really like it. Here, this is for you if you want it."

"Thank you so very much," the lady said with a rickety voice.

"Umm, Miss Lady, my sister Margaret has somethin' to tell you," I stammered.

"Oh, how lovely. Are y'all the twins that sat behind me in church today?" she asked.

"Uh, yes, Ma'am, we are," we both uttered at the same time.

"Margaret has to tell you somethin'," I blurted.

"Well, Kat has somethin' to give you. Get it out of your purse, Kat."

"Oh, you do. How nice of you girls," the old lady answered.

"Yes, Ma'am. I don't know how, but somehow this ol' eyeball fell into my purse and I think it belongs to your dead fox. Betcha can glue it back in somehow, ya think?" I suggested as I carefully handed her the fox's eyeball.

Overjoyed, the old lady exclaimed, "Oh, my! I noticed when I got home from church that my fox stole was missing an eye. I didn't know where I had lost it. Isn't it lucky that it landed in your purse? Thank you so kindly, girls, for returning it to me."

"Yes, Ma'am, it *was* lucky, wasn't it? But can I ask you somethin'? Why does that fox bite its tail? It looks funny doin' that. And did you find it on the side of the road and stuff it? Just wonderin'," I asked in rapid succession. I tend to talk a lot when I'm nervous.

The purple-haired lady grinned broadly, answering, "Well, let's see. The teeth act as a clasp. And, no, I didn't pick it off the side of the road and stuff it. I bought it from a fur dealer in Memphis. Now is there anything else you girls want to know?"

I quickly asked, "Do you know why they call it a stole? It's not stolen, is it?"

Amused at our question and giggling in a nice old lady way, she answered, "I'm not quite sure why it's called a stole, but I know for certain that it's not stolen."

"Oh, yes, Ma'am. Our brother said it wasn't stolen, so we figured you didn't steal it. You sure have pretty hair. We like it that color. It's dyed isn't it? Mama said you dyed it that color and it's real pretty. Ice cream's good, isn't it? Well, we gotta go. Glad you got your eyeball back," Margaret stammered as the two of us turned and skipped away, hand in hand.

"She was a real, sweet old lady, wasn't she?" I said as we loped away with our now clear consciences.

Before we could reach the outside door, Mama stopped us asking, "What were you two talking to Mrs. Smith about?"

"Uh, Margaret just wanted to tell her we think her dyed hair is pretty," I explained sheepishly. We turned and ran for the outside door.

REINDEER PAWS

Christmas in 1956 was special for the five King kids. We were spending Christmas in our new home on Park Drive. We pestered Mama about Santa Claus, despite Christmas being several weeks away. She finally relented, loaded five eager kids in the family sedan, and off we went to see jolly ol' St. Nick. When we arrived, we could see him perched on his large chair, surrounded by several elfin helpers. He listened to an endless parade of awed little ones as they each shared their wishes. Fidgeting, we awaited our turn to crawl up on Santa's lap so we could go over our list of all the fun stuff we wanted for Christmas.

Counting down the days until Christmas was the hardest part. That year, Christmas Eve seemed the longest day of the year!

Kat and I were behind closed doors in the bedroom we shared. We were sitting on the hard wooden floor playing jacks when Kat suddenly asked, "Whatcha think Santa will bring us tonight? I hope I get some marbles and we surely could use some new jacks." Before I could respond, she added, "And a kick ball and gun and holster set. You know, Santa will bring us everything we want if we're good and I've been *real, real* good this year, Don't 'cha think?"

I jerked my head up surprised at that statement and reminded her, "You weren't so good when you made Bill feel really bad when he lost to you playin' marbles. You made him feel terrible losin' to a girl. And you weren't so good when you told our teacher you read a whole book in one day. And what about the time you stuck my finger in that ol' fox's eye and it fell out? Or what about the other day when..."

"Okay. Okay," Kat admitted, interrupting me rudely. "Don't keep goin' on and on. But that was two or three weeks ago. I've been real good since then."

I rebutted, "Well, yeah, I guess so. But today you picked a fight with Bill and got us both in trouble."

"Well, that doesn't count cause it's too late for Santa to find out 'bout that," she argued smugly.

"Yeah, but that's why we're stuck here in this room instead of gettin' Santa's cookies and milk ready. Betcha Kirk and Bill are havin' fun fixin' his snack. But I guess you've been pretty good and I've been good, too."

Kat agreed, looking down at the floor, "You're always good. Only time you get in trouble is when you're with me and both of us get blamed for everything. Think Santa will bring you everything you want?" Her mood changing, she quipped, "Sure hope I get a kick ball and you can play with me."

"Okay. I'll share my paper dolls with you if Santa brings me some."

"Naw, you don't have to share 'em. But if you get some candy, I'll let you share that," Kat said and grinned.

Just then the bedroom door opened and Mama announced supper was ready. We jumped to our feet, ready to eat because Santa would be arriving soon after supper was over. As soon as we finished eating, we raced for the bath tubs, bathed, and then hurriedly donned our winter pajamas. We could hardly wait for Mama to read our favorite Christmas Eve story, *The Night Before Christmas*, by Clement C. Moore.

We gathered in the living room at Mama's feet, as she and Daddy settled onto the sofa. I saw Allan look up expectantly, wide-eyed. He hung on to every word, excited that Santa's visit was tonight, then interrupted when Mama showed the picture of the red-harnessed flying reindeer, exclaiming, "Rudolph flies? Me not know that."

Glancing at Allan with a gleam in her eye, Mama continued, calling each tiny reindeer by name. As she finished describing Santa's merry dimples, rosy cheeks and cherry-like nose, Kirk at age five fretted, "Santa won't come in my room, will he? I don't want him in my room lookin' at me."

Worried, two-year old Allan jumped into Daddy's lap, elf-like in his red-toed pajamas and continued the protestations before Mama could hush her unruly brood. He placed both hands on Daddy's face, forcing eye-to-eye contact. Uneasy, he cried, "Santa come to me room? Oooh, No. Me lock the door. Not let Santa in."

Mama grinned at Kirk and Allan's concerns. Then, spreading her arms wide, she calmly explained, "Santa only comes in here and puts your presents under the tree. He will not come into your rooms. We'll shut all bedroom doors so you will feel safe. Now, let's finish this story so you can get to bed."

Before Mama got another word out, Kat blurted, "Well, I wanna see Santa and see Rudolph fly onto our rooftop. I'm gonna stay up 'til he comes and see his reindeer fly." Silence reigned. Momentarily surprised, Kat looked at Mama, then Daddy. She realized her mistake, backtracked and in a soothing voice explained, "Allan, you silly goose, quit frettin'. Santa won't hurt you."

Mama and Daddy exchanged knowing glances before Daddy set the record straight. "Santa won't come until all five of you are asleep." Addressing Kirk's concerns first, he stared into her worried face and explained patiently, "Santa won't come into your bedrooms, but he will know if you're asleep. So, when we're finished with this bedtime story, it'll be time to go to sleep." He then addressed Allan directly, enunciating clearly each word, "Santa will leave your presents under the tree then get back into his sleigh. He will take his flying reindeer and go to someone else's house." Pausing to let those facts sink in, he then turned to Kat and tenderly stated, "You, my child, will close your eyes as soon as I tuck you in. I know you're excited. Santa and his reindeer have a lot of places to go tonight, so you must go to sleep quickly. Now, let's finish this story."

Older and wiser, brother Bill admonished, "Kat, you better go to sleep. If we don't get any presents 'cause you stayed awake, we'll all be mad at you and you won't have any toys or candy either."

"Now, no more talking," Mama directed, hoping to avoid further interruptions as she hurriedly resumed the bedtime story, impatient to get her charges in bed. When Santa closed with his jolly, "Happy Christmas to all and to all a good night," we all eagerly scrambled to our rooms, heads swimming with anticipation of what Santa would bring.

Crawling into bed, Daddy tucked us in, smiled and gently said, "Girls, you go to sleep. No talking. Remember, Santa won't come until you're asleep."

"Yes, Daddy, we'll go to sleep," we answered in unison.

As he shut the door, Daddy's last "Goodnight, girls," hit deaf ears as Kat jumped off the top bunk and quickly made her way to the window. She parted the curtains, determined to see Santa's arrival.

"Get back in bed and go to sleep or Santa won't ever come," I whispered, worried that Santa would skip our house if we were awake.

"Yes, he will, and I want to see his reindeer flyin' in the air. Don't you?" Kat said, not taking her eyes from the sky.

"Yeah, but what if Daddy's right and Santa won't come 'til we're asleep," I argued.

"Well," she said looking directly at me. Before she could finish her thought, we heard a noise on the roof top.

"Oh my gosh! Santa's here and I didn't get to see his reindeer. I looked away for just a second and missed seein' him. You think we could sneak out the door? I just gotta see his reindeer. Rudolph is my favorite, and I want to see if his red nose really does shine."

I explained patiently, "They're on the roof. You can't see 'em. And you better be quiet or Santa won't bring you anything."

Frustrated, Kat responded, "Okay. Okay! But it sounds like Santa is in the attic right above our room."

Both scared and excited, she jumped in bed with me and we held each other tight, too afraid to let go. I whispered, "Do you really think that's Santa?"

"Gotta be," Kat replied barely audible. "We better go to sleep right now. What if he comes in here and finds us still awake? Can I sleep down here with you? It's too scary up there on the top bunk. Come on, let's go to sleep," she insisted.

Not another word was said between us, but in our excitement, neither of us could fall asleep. The continuing noise of reindeer paws above us kept us wide-eyed. And just short minutes later, the noise ended and Santa and his reindeer were gone. In the darkness of the room, I sensed Kat's sniffling and shared her disappointment in missing Santa's reindeer.

But tomorrow, Christmas Day and Santa's gifts would push away regrets and make room for only happiness.

THE HORSE'S TAILS

From the time we were old enough to understand anything, we knew that our hair was a source of distress and concern for us as well as Mama. She was constantly at a loss as to what to do with our unruly messes, causing all of us many stressful moments. From our first birthday forward, Mama often referred to our hair as the horse's tails—not necessarily for its length, but because it was coarse, thick and lots of it—times two! As we grew older, we worried from one hairstyle to the next, wondering what "do" was soon to be in our future.

"Hardheaded" was another term used to describe us, and rightfully so—not in terms of stubbornness but in terms of being tough headed. One thing's for sure, we were not tender headed—not after what our scalps endured through the years. If it could be done to hair, it was done to ours, with one exception—shaving our heads. And we weren't so sure that shaving our heads wasn't a consideration at times, as Mama shook her head often in bewilderment. We had pigtails, ponytails, page boys, the flip, fros and home perms—lots of home perms—all in the hunt to find a solution to tame the horse's tails. It seemed as though every few months a new 'do' was in the works.

One Sunday morning in late August, 1957, just before we were to begin the fourth grade, I woke and began our Sunday ritual with the same question coming from the top bunk.

"Reckon we gotta go to Sunday school today?" I asked Margaret.

"Don't know. I hear Mama in the kitchen gettin' breakfast ready, so I guess so," Margaret replied.

I scrambled to the foot of the bed to pull the curtains aside to see the sun shining bright.

"Looks like a great day to play outside. I'd like to climb that tree again. Did you see me climb all the way to the top of it? You only got half way up and couldn't get back down. You need to go ask Mama if we gotta go to church. Maybe we can stay home and play outside like we've done all summer," I offered, planning the day for us.

"I'm gonna get Allan to ask her," Margaret countered.

Before we could put our plan into action, Mama called from the kitchen, "Breakfast in five minutes. Don't be late."

I jumped down from the top bunk, and we headed for Allan's room.

Allan was still asleep as I shook his small body awake, whispering, "Go ask Mama if we gotta go to Sunday school today. Beg her to let us stay home. I'll teach you how to climb that tree if you do. Come on. Get up. Let's go. And don't tell her we put you up to this."

Standing at the doorway to the kitchen, the three of us peered in to see Mama placing breakfast on the table.

Allan looked at me and I mouthed, "Go on," as I gently pushed him forward.

"Mama, do we hafta go to Sunday school today? Can we stay home and climb trees? Please Mama, can we? Kat said she'll teach me how to climb trees if we get to stay home. Can we, Mama?" Allan pleaded.

"No," came the short reply from Mama.

"Why, Mama, why can't we?" Allan continued begging.

"Because I said so," came her pat response. "Now go get everybody else to come eat breakfast. Hurry. Go on," she continued.

Allan ran back to us as we stood just outside the kitchen and yelled, "Mama said 'no' and we hafta go to church. She said to come on and eat. I gotta tell Kirk and Bill that Mama said breakfast is ready to eat."

We sauntered into the kitchen, not looking at Mama, and sat down to eat breakfast.

"Y'all didn't put your three-year old brother up to asking that, did you?" she asked turning from the stove to make eye contact with us.

Surprised at our appearance she exclaimed, "My goodness. What happened to your hair? It looks like a horse's tail all tangled up. Did y'all sleep upside down? I've got to do something with your hair. It's just too unruly."

We looked at each other and realized Mama's concern. We knew pain and suffering would come shortly after breakfast when she combed out the tangles and put our hair in either ponytails or pigtails.

"As soon as you finish breakfast, go to the girls' bathroom and wait for me to brush out those tangles," she directed. "Do you want pigtails or ponytails?" she asked.

"Ponytails," we blurted out in unison.

"We'll see. Now hurry up and finish eating. It'll take some time to comb out that mess of tangles," Mama sighed.

"You'll find your brush in the boys' bathroom. I used it just a few minutes ago before I came to the breakfast table," Bill offered.

I glared at Bill, and picked at the food to prolong the inevitable. I mumbled in a low voice to Margaret, "Slow down. Don't eat so fast. It's gonna really hurt when she starts combin' out those tangles. I'll go second."

Mama must have overheard my comment because she directed, "Katherine, you're almost through, so put your plate in the sink and go back and start brushing out those tangles. I'll do your hair first."

"Yes, Ma'am," I muttered.

Before Mama arrived, Margaret joined me in the bathroom. "Whatcha lookin' for?" Margaret asked me as I stood on the toilet lid peering into Mama's makeup drawer.

"Mama's brush. I'm not gonna use the one Bill used. I wanna get most of these tangles out before Mama gets here."

"Right. Give it to me when you're finished. Sure hope it's a ponytail and not pigtails," Margaret commented.

All conversation stopped when Mama entered the small bathroom, pointed a comb at me, and said, "Let's get started. Just sit down on the side of the tub and look up at me." Combing through my bangs, she continued, "I think your bangs are too long. We'll cut them this afternoon after lunch. Now turn around and put your feet in the tub so I can part your hair. Remember, sit still; try not to move, so we won't have to start over."

As I obeyed Mama's instructions, I glanced at Margaret and handed her the brush. Our fate was sealed—pigtails it was! Working tirelessly, Mama combed my hair free of tangles and made a perfectly straight part from bangs to nape before binding the tightly formed pigtails with rubber bands directly behind each ear.

I cringed, teary-eyed, as the suffering lasted ten minutes before I was on my way out the door to dress for Sunday school. leaving Margaret to face the torture chamber alone.

Mama's final instruction to me directed, "Katherine, try not to mess up your hair getting dressed. If you do, I'll have to start over. Understand?"

Looking Mama straight into her face I answered, "Oh, yes, Ma'am, I understand."

Ten minutes later, Margaret entered the bedroom with a look of startled surprise on her face.

I asked, "What did Mama do to you? She pulled your pigtails so tight that it stretched your face backward."

Margaret retorted, "Well, she did the same thing to you. Go look in the mirror and see for yourself."

I left for the bathroom to look in the mirror and ran into Bill, who teased, "You look like you've had your skin stretched. Kirk and Allan, come see how weird Kat looks."

Before my siblings could gather to stare at me, I retreated to our bedroom, slammed the door in Bill's face and asked, "What's stretched skin? I know it's not good 'cause Bill is pointin' and laughin' at me and callin' me weird."

"I don't know, but it must look like *us,*" Margaret answered.

After church and lunch were over, we found ourselves once again face to face with Mama in the girls' bathroom—this time for the bang trimming venture.

I blurted out, "You go first. I had to go first this mornin'."

"That's because Mama chose you to go first," Margaret answered.

"Yes, and I think you should go first again, Katherine. Sit on the toilet and let's get started," Mama directed.

I slumped onto the toilet as Mama draped a towel under my chin, explaining, "Hold this so it will catch the loose hair when I cut it. Now sit up straight and be still so this won't take me all afternoon to do."

Margaret watched from the side of the tub as Mama tilted my chin upward, ran the comb under the running water, then plastered the bangs to my forehead. It seemed to me the towel was put to better use catching the excess water as it trickled down my face. I closed my eyes as Mama began snipping. Between snips, I looked into Margaret's face for her reaction, which was never good. I wrinkled my forehead and raised my eyebrows to see if I could tell what was wrong. Mama took a step back to assess her handiwork, then started again trying to even out both sides.

A second assessment brought with it an admonishment from Mama, "Katherine, be still. Stop wiggling. The more you wiggle the longer this will take."

"Yeah, if you'd quit lookin' up to see what Mama's doin', your bangs wouldn't be so short," Margaret interjected.

"How short are they? Are they *really, really* short? Can I look in the mirror now?" I whined.

"Not just yet. Let me finish," Mama replied as she raised the scissors to continue trimming.

Hair continued to fall into the hand-held towel as I thought, *Oh, please let this be the last time. If she doesn't stop I won't have any bangs left at all.*

Mama must have thought the same thing as she stepped back and commented, "Guess this will have to do. I don't think I can get them any shorter. Okay, Katherine, I'm finished. You can get up now and shake out the towel in the trash can and then give it to Margaret."

I jumped off the toilet seat and gasped as I looked into the mirror. Tears welled up in my eyes as I left the bathroom without saying a single word.

I stumbled over Allan, Bill, and Kirk sitting in the doorway. For all to hear, Bill, the critic, announced,

"Mama, I think the right side is longer than the left. Don't you wanna fix that?"

I pushed Bill aside and with my fist in his face, mouthed, "You're gonna be sorry if you say another word." I shut the bedroom door behind me, a final warning to *all* that I wanted to be left alone.

Not long afterward, Margaret joined me sitting on the bedroom floor. She mirrored my image—identical results. I couldn't believe how short her bangs were. "You look funny," I said.

"Yeah, I know. I'm lookin' at you," Margaret countered, and we started laughing.

"What if we raise our eyebrows? That'll make the bangs come down some, won't it?"

Staring at me as I demonstrated the intended look, Margaret replied, "We can't go around all day lookin' like that. You look like someone just jumped out at you and said *boo,* scarin' you to death. How long do you think it'll take for 'em to grow back?"

"Too long," I sighed. *Much too long,* I thought.

Momentarily, Mama opened the bedroom door, grinned at us and made an astonishing statement, "I've made up my mind. It's time to get your hair cut. I don't have time to deal with this every day so I'm going to call Collie Mae and schedule haircuts."

I leapt to my feet, shocked, and asked, "How short? I don't want it too short."

"We'll see, Katherine," came Mama's reply as she left, closing the door and leaving us to fret and ponder the possibilities. We loved to have our long hair put into pony tails and pigtails, no matter how much it hurt pulling the rubber bands out each night.

"Maybe we're just goin' in for a trim, like Mama does our bangs," I offered as I swished my pigtails back and forth.

"Maybe, but look at what her idea of trimmin' bangs is. And she said *haircut*, didn't she?" Margaret questioned.

"Yeah, she said hair*cut!*" I said, getting nervous.

Then a week went by and we didn't hear any more about a haircut and hoped that Mama had forgotten all about it. We certainly weren't going to remind her.

As our family of seven gathered around the small black and white RCA television the following Saturday night to watch *The Miss America Pageant*, we gazed at the beauties strolling down the runway in Atlantic City.

As Burt Parks introduced each contestant, we found ourselves focusing mainly on the different hairstyles, desperately hoping to find one that would address our particular hair problems. We jumped up and down, clapping loudest for Miss Mississippi every time she appeared. She was, by far, the most beautiful of all.

During the first commercial break, Mama popped some popcorn and we ate hungrily, waiting for the commercials to end. As Mama put another bowl of popcorn in front of us, a commercial caught her attention. We looked up from eating popcorn to see a Toni Home Perm ad on TV. We oohed and aahed at the hairstyles of the models. The girls in the ad had the prettiest hair, some long and some short, but all had soft, bouncy curls.

Then there was a set of beautiful identical twins. We had to guess which one had the Toni. The twin sisters told us that Toni Home Perms are fast and easy and can be done in the privacy of our own home. And, with a Toni Home Perm we could control the amount of curls—tight or loose and very soft—so many miracles in one small box! The lasting impression was… we could look just like Miss America. Hah! At least we could dream.

"Wow. Wonder how they get their hair like that? Ours is just straight as a board," I said looking at my own droopy locks.

Mama nodded, adding, "Maybe some curls are what you girls need. I'll check with Collie Mae when I call for your haircuts."

We looked at each other, wondering if Toni Home Perms were in our future.

Sure enough, the following Friday the three of us journeyed to Collie Mae's Beauty Shop.

On the way, Mama tried to prepare us for what was about to happen. "Girls, I've talked to Collie Mae and she seems to think your hair is too long and thick for a perm. So we're going to get your hair cut short and then we'll get a perm."

Seated in the back seat, we were shocked to hear this news as we looked into each other's face.

Margaret begged, "Please, Mama, don't let her cut our hair too short."

Nothing else was said as Mama parked the car. We entered the beauty shop and Mama had a private conversation with Collie Mae before turning to us with instructions, "Girls, I'm going up the street for a few things. Do as Miss Collie Mae says. I've told her what to do. I'll be back shortly."

As Mama left the shop we watched as Miss Collie Mae teased some old lady's bluish-gray hair into a rat's nest before covering it up. We had never seen or smelled so much chemical stink as when this lady with cotton outlining her face bent close to us to select a magazine. I pinched my nose as she turned her back and heard Margaret gasp for air. We looked at each other, stunned, as we stared at women sitting around in chairs sporting different stages of hair beautification. Within minutes, Collie Mae was through with the rat-nested woman and was motioning for me to come over to sit in the barber chair.

I stood but couldn't move and finally blurted, "Margaret's goin' first. Go on, Margaret. Miss Collie Mae wants you first."

"Okay, Margaret, come on, you can go first," Collie Mae said, extending a hand in Margaret's direction.

"See, I told you to go first and Miss Collie Mae agrees. Go on now," I insisted, pointing to the chair.

Margaret glared at me as she made her way to the chair. Facing the mirror, she practically disappeared under the apron that was draped around her shoulders. All I could see was her staring at me, gritting her teeth. I grinned back and Miss Collie Mae turned Margaret to face me where I sat in the barber chair beside her. Having just realized the chairs would spin, I began to slowly turn around and around to avoid looking at Margaret.

"Miss Collie Mae, please don't cut our hair too short. We want to keep our pony tails," Margaret begged.

As soon as the words were out of Margaret's mouth, Miss Collie Mae picked up the scissors and cut the rubber band.

"Oh, Miss Collie Mae, Mama never cuts the rubber bands. She pulls them out of our hair at night and uses them next day," I explained.

Collie Mae looked at me and replied, "It's okay, girls. You won't need them anymore," as she snipped eight inches of hair off in one swift motion.

I stopped spinning the chair and starred in disbelief as the hair cascaded to the floor. Seeing my mouth agape, Margaret tried to peek sideways into the mirror, but it was impossible for her to see what had happened.

Miming to Margaret, I started patting my hair, hoping she would pick up on the gesture. She must have known from the look on my face that her hair was gone as tears began to trickle down her cheeks.

I'm next, was all I could think of.

As Collie Mae finished cutting Margaret's hair, she explained, "Now, I'm going to layer your hair and thin it out."

"What does that mean?" I asked.

"Well, I can't do anything about how coarse your hair is, but I can thin it out so it won't be so thick. Then maybe your Mama will have an easier time fixing it," Collie Mae explained.

"What does layered mean?" Margaret inquired.

"You'll see when I'm finished. It'll make getting a perm easier," she answered.

Within minutes, I had to crawl into that chair. As strands of hair fell to the floor, I cried. The results were identical. Now instead of long, straight, thick, coarse hair we had maybe three inches of coarse hair that stuck out in all directions. We looked like we had just stuck our finger into a light socket.

When Mama returned, she smiled at us, paid Collie Mae, and marched us to the car.

Once in the back seat, we were again stunned at the announcement Mama made, "Girls, while you were getting your haircuts, I walked down to Gathright-Reed Drug Store to buy two Toni Home Permanent kits so we can curl your hair tomorrow."

"Can't we let Miss Collie Mae do it?" Margaret pleaded, adding, "She's done lots of 'em and you've never even done one."

"No, we can't afford to pay Collie Mae to do two perms. She says it's not hard and we'll just follow the directions in the box. You girls look cute with short hair."

Not another word was spoken on the trip home as Margaret kept running her fingers through her short, thin hair, not believing what she was feeling. I sat with my elbows on my knees, cradling my face, silently crying.

Mama stopped by the Tatum's house to pick up Bill, Kirk, and Allan, who were playing outside when we drove up. She took time to speak to her best friend, Dorothy Lee, as we cowered in the back seat, dreading our sibling's stares and jeers. But none came as they jumped in the back seat with us.

Kirk commented, "I like your hair short."

Allan added, "Me, too. It's really short."

Bill chimed in with, "Mama told Mrs. Dorothy Lee that she's givin' you a perm tomorrow. It'll look much better after she curls it."

Those words gave us little comfort. Our long, straight hair was gone and now we had to withstand getting curls tomorrow. It just wasn't fair, not fair at all. Tears again pooled in our eyes as we wiped them away before they could trickle down our faces.

After breakfast the next morning, Mama opened up the Toni Home Perm box and set all the supplies on the kitchen table. We looked at the words on the bottles: neutralizer, solution. What did they mean? She placed several boxes of pink curlers and lots of cotton and towels next to the bottles.

"Who's going first?" Mama asked.

"Margaret is," I answered firmly.

"It's your turn to go first. I got my hair cut first, remember?" Margaret whined.

"Okay, Margaret. It doesn't matter. Both of you are getting a perm so you may as well go first," Mama explained.

Margaret sighed, "Yes, Ma'am," as she glared at me.

I was hoping Mama would work out any problems she'd have on Margaret's hair before she got to me.

Mama draped a towel around Margaret's shoulders, handing her the corners of the towel, saying, "Hold this tightly at your neck so the solution won't seep down your back through to your clothes. I'll need you to hand me one of those small square tissues before I put each curler in. Katherine, you hand me the largest curlers first, then we'll use the smaller ones around the sides and back. Now, let's get started."

Mama snipped off the tip of the solution bottle, parted off a small amount of hair, wrapped the tissue paper around that section of hair, wound the hair tightly around the curler, snapping it in place before applying the solution. Curler after curler was snapped into place until Margaret's entire head was filled with pink curlers cushioned with white tissue paper. She smelled just like the lady at Miss Collie Mae's.

"I don't think you're gonna look like the pretty ladies in the Miss America ad. I'm sure they didn't look like this," I declared.

"Well, you're next so we'll see if you look any better," Margaret snipped.

"Okay, girls. That's enough. Margaret, I'm through rolling your hair. Now I'm going to put the remainder of this solution on, so hold the towel tightly around your face. Then I'm going to set the timer and get started on Katherine's hair."

Mama became quite proficient with the curlers and it took only half the time to roll up my hair. I knew what I must look like because I was staring at Margaret. Having set the second timer, Mama left the kitchen. As the timer slowly ticked away our destiny, we began whispering about the outcome.

"Whatcha think we're gonna look like?" Margaret asked.

Before I could answer, Bill walked into the kitchen, starred at us, and teased, "I read the instructions. Did y'all know you're gonna smell like this for three months? This smell doesn't go away so y'all are gonna stink for a long time."

I chased Bill from the kitchen, yet I wondered if he was telling the truth.

At this particular moment, I was ready to ditch the Miss America look. Turning to Margaret, I ordered, "Pick up the paper that came inside the box and see if it says we're gonna stink for three months."

Before Margaret could read the instructions, Kirk and Allan appeared in the doorway, gawking at us. Allan had his mouth and nose covered with his hands, barely breathing between his fingers.

He asked, mumbling innocently, "Kat, which one is you, and what stinks so bad?"

"Yeah, it smells like the stuff Mama cleans the floors with," our six-year old sister, Kirk, added.

"I'm gonna tell Mama y'all are in here botherin' us, so you better get outta here before she comes back," I threatened.

Hearing Mama's footsteps coming down the hall, Allan and Kirk raced in the opposite direction, squealing, "pee-yew" and giggling at our distress.

As the timer dinged indicating Margaret's hair was done, I asked, "Mama, Bill said our hair is gonna stink for three months. Is that right?"

"Of course not. Bill's just teasing you. Now, let's get your hair rinsed, Margaret, and get the curlers out and the neutralizer applied. Come on over here and stick your head under the faucet," Mama instructed.

As soon as Mama finished with Margaret's hair and wrapped it in a towel, the dinger rang again and it was my time to finish up, repeating the steps Margaret had just endured. The cool water felt good on my burning scalp.

"Keep the towel wrapped tightly around your head until I'm finished with Katherine's hair," Mama directed.

Putting the finishing touches to my hair, Mama toweled it dry and pointing to Margaret said, "Take the towel off now and let's see what you girls look like." She seemed pleased, "I've never seen so many curls. Now go outside and we'll let it dry naturally."

"Can we see it first?" I asked.

"Yeah, I wanna see how it looks," Margaret added.

"You'll have to wait until it dries before you can tell anything. Now, run on outside," Mama directed.

Margaret and I went out back and sat on the picnic table. Bill, Kirk, and Allan were already there waiting for us to come out.

"Do we look the same?" I asked Bill.

"Yeah, you both got lots of wet curls," Bill replied.

"Yeah, lots of curls, and you still stink," Allan added, waving his hands back and forth to clear the air.

"You can't wash your hair for three days so y'all are gonna stink like that for a long time," Bill teased.

"Oh, it's not so bad and you got lots of pretty curls now like mine," Kirk offered.

We looked at each other and I said, "Yeah, but your curls are soft and bouncy. Ours are wound up so tight, like springs ready to uncoil but nothin' happens. They just stay wound up."

We sat there watching each other's hair dry, hoping for a good outcome. About an hour later we ran our fingers through short, curly hair and raced inside to the bathroom mirror. Looking back at us were strangers with frizzy hair. What happened to the soft bouncing curls—not exactly Miss Americas—not even close.

"Looks like someone stuck a Brillo pad on our heads, doesn't it?" I asked.

"Yeah," Margaret said turning her head from side to side.

"But, the good thing is we still look alike." I added, "That didn't change. I think we look more alike than ever and that's a good thing. I hate it. I miss our ponytails. But at least Mama won't be pullin' our hair out with rubber bands anymore."

Margaret interjected, "I tried puttin' a bobby pin in it, but it sprang back out, so we won't be able to pin it down."

I sighed, "Oh, well. Come on, let's go out and play, or we could go see if Tarzan is on TV. We've wasted enough time messin' with our hair."

Years later, we realized that we had the original *'fro*. The 'fros of the '60s and '70s were imitations of *our* 1957 hairstyle. We had the *'fro* before the *'fro* became a *'fro*, making a fashion statement for others to follow for decades to come! And so it went, year after year, seeking the perfect hairdo for our "horse's tails." Every year, when the *Miss America Pageant* aired, we looked closely at the Toni Home Perm ads, thinking, possibly, just possibly, another perm would be in our future and maybe, just maybe, *this* year would be a better 'hairdo' year for us.

SHARING—OR NOT

According to Kat, we shared everything. According to me, Kat only shared what she did not want for herself. Conversely, I shared everything I had without reservations. And so it went.

Birthday presents are a good example of sharing—or not sharing. As little girls, we always celebrated our birthdays with a backyard party. Birthday parties in the 1950s were very simple. Themes did not dominate the parties. There were no custom-made cakes. We did not go in groups to the picture show. We did not rent the skating rink and invite 50 of our best friends, and there were no fast food restaurants to cater our parties. As I said, birthday parties were simple—one-hour backyard celebrations. We entertained ourselves by playing chase, climbing trees, jumping rope, competing in hopscotch, shooting marbles, playing jacks, playing red rover, or pinning the tail on the donkey. We opened gifts and ate homemade cake—always a two-layer chocolate cake with chocolate icing, topped with vanilla ice cream. From beginning to end, one hour lapsed.

Just prior to our tenth birthday in 1958, we began making plans for a backyard party. The Saturday before our birthday we were sitting on the floor of our bedroom. With legs stretched out, Kat and I were writing down our birthday wish list.

"I really hope someone will give us a new yo-yo," Kat said as she paused before writing it down on her list. "How do you spell 'yo'?" she questioned.

Paying little attention to her I mumbled, "I hope we get some pop beads. You know they're real popular now. Did you see the ones Debbie had on yesterday? I really want some of 'em, don't you? We can share 'em, you know. I can wear 'em one day and you can the next."

"Some what? I don't know what you're talkin' about. You mean those snap bead things? Why would you want somethin' like that?" Kat asked irritated. "But we could use a new jump rope. Ours is worn out. Don't 'cha want a new jump rope?"

At the sound of the door opening, we looked up from the Sears Roebuck catalogue to find Mama entering our room.

"Girls, we need to talk about planning your birthday party. Since school is out next Friday and your birthday is Saturday, let's go ahead and have the party on your birthday at 2:00. You may invite ten guests."

"Each? That's great! Here are my ten friends. Denny, and Rita and Debbie, and," Kat said excitedly but was quickly cut off.

"No, you can have ten friends in all. Not ten each," Mama said firmly. "Listen quietly while I tell you the rest of the plans. Your brothers and sister are three of your guests, so that leaves you with seven others you may invite," Mama continued.

"But we don't wanna have any boys at the party. Why do Bill and Allan get to come? That's not fair," Kat said a little too strongly and with a scowl on her face.

"Your brothers will be at the party or you will not have one," Mama retorted quickly.

"Okay, okay, okay they can come. It's okay if they come," I said, trying to sound convincing to deflect Mama from Kat's loud whine.

"Now let me finish with what I came in here to say," Mama said in a matter-of-fact tone. "I want to know who you are inviting. Clear the list with me before you make the calls. I will bake a chocolate cake with chocolate icing."

"Can we have some chocolate ice cream on top?" Kat asked.

"No. But you may have some vanilla ice cream," Mama said firmly. "Do you understand?"

"Oh, yes, Ma'am," Kat quickly responded.

"Please let me finish, girls. Monday I'll go to Morgan and Lindsey's 5 and 10 cent store and buy ten party favors. You both need to agree on what you want to give as favors. You will also need to clean your room completely before we have guests over, in case they come back here to your room. Now do you two understand everything I have said?"

"Oh, yes, Ma'am," we said in unison. "We understand."

Mama left the room abruptly and we sat staring at each other, not believing all that had just taken place.

"We have so much to do to get ready for our party," I said looking at Kat. "Who do you want to invite? It's going to be hard to pick just seven isn't it?"

"Yeah, it's 'cause we're wastin' three friends we can't invite 'cause of Kirk, Allan and Bill. That's just not fair," Kat sighed. "What do you want for favors?" I think we should give everyone one of those big red, wax lips. When you get tired of wearin' it, you can chew it like gum. Takes a long time to finally chew 'em all up. That's what I wanna give. What do you think?"

"Well, it's definitely not wax lips," I responded with a smirk on my face. "Why don't we give everyone paper dolls? They're lots of fun to play with. Don't you think so?"

"Paper dolls?" Kat asked as if she was insulted by my suggestion. "That's a borin' gift. That's a sissy favor." The paper dolls were dismissed. "Do you think our friends will bring us two presents? Or just one present for us to share? I hope we get two."

"I'm sure we'll only get one to share. You know we never get two. Remember what Mama always tells us, 'Most of your friends think of y'all as a single unit—The King Twins. This means that y'all have to share each present you get.' But that's okay 'cause we can share with each other, right?" I responded.

"If we have to, but maybe they'll bring two presents this year. And then we won't have to share," Kat grumbled under her breath. "We gotta make a list out of friends to invite. You write down all the names and then we'll figure out which ones we wanna come."

Making a long list of potential guests, we chose our seven closest friends.

"Come on, let's take this list to Mama before she changes her mind and only lets us invite five. And Kirk, Allan and Bill will be three of 'em," Kat said as she jumped up, sprinted for the door and down the hall to the kitchen.

Slowing down at the kitchen door, we strolled to Mama's side.

"Here's our list, Mama," Kat said, as she stretched out her arm and handed it over.

Mama looked at the list and nodded approvingly until she came to the party favors. "Wax lips? Are you girls sure you want to give wax lips?"

"I didn't wanna give 'em. That was Kat's idea. I wanna give paper dolls. Don't you think that's better?" I said, hoping Mama would agree with me.

"Since you girls can't agree on this, I'll pick out something myself," Mama insisted.

She also took this opportunity to add a few more restrictions for the party. "Now you must plan the entertainment. Make sure everything you do can be done outside. I don't want y'all running in and out of this house. And, if it's raining, we'll have it under the car port. Is that clear?"

"Yes, Ma'am. We'll plan everything, and, yes, Ma'am, I really wish you would get the wax lips as favors. All our friends really love 'em," Kat answered before I had a chance to speak.

"Well, we'll see, Katherine. I really don't want red wax all over the sidewalk. So let me think about it," Mama responded.

Back in our room Kat appointed herself as chair of the entertainment committee by stating, "This is what we're gonna do. We're gonna jump rope, climb trees, and shoot marbles."

As the only other committee member, I offered alternative activities, "My friends don't wanna do that. They wanna cut out paper dolls, practice cheers, or play house with our dolls."

Each of us thought we had the perfect party plan and neither would compromise. Therefore, the competition of recruiting friends began as soon as each friend arrived at the party the following Saturday afternoon.

Anticipating the arrival of our guests, we were permanently perched on the front steps thirty minutes before party time. As the hour drew near, we kept a close watch for cars turning into our long gravel driveway. At the first sound of gravel crunching beneath the tires, Kat sent me on a bogus mission declaring, "Mama's callin' you from the back patio. Better not keep her waitin'."

Leaping from the steps I hurried to the back to see what Mama wanted of me. But she wasn't back there. I found her in the kitchen and asked her what she needed me to do.

Confused, Mama said, "I didn't need you for anything, but, while you are here, you can take the pitcher of Kool-Aid out back to the picnic table."

I glanced through the large picture window to see Kat greeting our first guest. Getting out of the car was one of our best friends, Rita. I rushed out the back door and placed the pitcher of Kool-Aid on the table. I glanced up to see Kat and Rita coming around the side of the house toward me.

"Happy birthday, Margaret," came the greeting from Rita. "It's really hot out here today. Can we go inside and get some water?"

"You can ask Mama when she comes out if you want to."

"No, that's okay. I'll just drink some of that cold Kool-Aid," she countered.

"You stay here with Rita and I'll go see who else is here. I'll bring 'em around here and you take the presents and put 'em on the table," Kat said as she sprinted back toward the driveway.

As our friends were dropped off, Kat recruited each to join her at play. But rounding the corner of the house with the seventh and final guest, Kat was shocked to see that everyone was in a circle playing house with our dolls.

Jumping into the circle, Kat asked, "Who wants to play red rover? Let's split up into two teams and play."

When no one responded, she wandered over to the picnic table to look at the gifts laid out neatly. Every gift was wrapped in pink paper with pink, frilly ribbons or bows. She was very disappointed, since it seemed to her, that not a single guest brought two gifts. Also, most of the guests were more inclined to play the lady-like games.

Much to her dismay, Kat only had one trump card left to play, and she wasn't sure how it would play out. She silently wondered if the gifts would be something she would enjoy or discard into my stack. Watching our friends playing in my camp, Kat eyeballed each and every present set before her. She began to have a sinking feeling. Would there be a single gift just for her or would all of them be rejects?

Upon initial inspection of the wrapped gifts, Kat thought she saw what could just possibly be a baseball glove, a kickball, a cap gun, a jump rope, and a deck of cards, and hoped the rest of the gifts would also be something that was on her wish list.

Within minutes, Mama came through the back door with cake and ice cream. Everyone scrambled for the picnic table to get a better look. Opening gifts was delayed by serving ice cream and cake. When it came time to blow out the ten candles, we were both sitting on the picnic bench beside the cake ready for Mama to give us the signal. As our friends stood around the table singing "Happy Birthday," Kat pushed me aside and with one big puff of wind the candles were extinguished.

As the birthday girls, we always received the first two pieces of cake. I got the end piece with all the icing and Kat got the next piece. This was the slowest part of the party—the event before opening the gifts. Since we had to wait for all guests to finish eating, this was an especially anxious time for us.

Kat's trump card was to open all gifts addressed, "To Kat and Margaret." Those hopes were dashed when Mama intervened, handing out the gifts to us in turn. As she reached in our direction with the first present, Kat quickly tried to snatch it. However, Mama insisted on handing it to me, deflating Kat's hopes.

Carefully removing the bow I thought, *I hope it's something both of us can play with. If it's something Kat really likes she'll keep it for herself.*

Before the paper was torn away and the white box opened, Kat whispered in my ear, "I bet that is a baseball glove. I can't wait to see it. You can throw balls to me and I can catch 'em. I hope it's for a left-hander."

I exclaimed, "Oh look, it's a soft baby doll and blanket. Thank you, Debbie. Thank you. Thank you. This is just what we wanted isn't it, Kat."

"Who gave us this thing?" Kat asked, visibly disappointed.

Mama, now standing behind Kat, whispered for her to be sweet and thank Debbie for the doll.

Kat did so reluctantly. But now it was her turn to open one. She reached out for the gift that looked like a kickball.

Looking over her shoulder Kat asked, "Can I open this one next?"

Mama nodded her approval. Kat tore off the ribbon and ripped off the paper as fast as she could. The box top had a picture of a ball on it.

"It's a ball," she said before she saw the actual gift. When she opened the box she was shocked to see something quite different. She quickly amended her statement by saying, "I mean it's a box full of doll clothes. Wow. Thanks." That's all she could think of to say.

"Say 'thank you' to Denny," Mama urged us both in her sweetest but insistent tone.

"Thank you so much, Denny. We can put these clothes on the baby doll we just got," I added excitedly as I picked up one of the pink dresses to see if it would fit our new doll.

"Yeah, thanks, Den," Kat added dejectedly.

I carefully placed the box of doll clothes with the baby doll in a stack that I knew would be all mine.

The third gift was placed in front of me. It was the smallest present on the table.

"I'm pretty sure that is a cap gun," Kat mumbled so only I could hear.

With that thought in mind, I hurried to open the small gift, hoping it would be something just for her. After all, I already had the doll and clothes.

We both stared at the white box and its contents. Written across the cover of the pink gift was DIARY. We then stared at each other.

I knew Kat must be thinking, *This is the most useless gift so far. A DIARY!*

With a look of disgust and shock, Kat reread the gift tag to see which friend had given her, or rather them, this awful present. No matter, since a diary was useless to Kat, it quickly became my property, whether I wanted it or not. Kat had no plans to write anything down—then or ever. "What a wasted gift!" she mumbled. "Here you can have it."

So she shared it with me. This was Kat's definition of sharing. Three gifts opened and all for me. I was really enjoying our party. Surely there would be something for Kat, but it was looking doubtful from her viewpoint.

Mama placed the fourth gift in front of Kat.

"I betcha this is a jump rope," she whispered in my ear.

She ripped it open in a matter of seconds only to find some pearly-white pop beads.

"Ugh!" Kat said, not hiding her disappointment any longer.

"What did *you say*, Katherine?" Mama asked.

"I said here, Margaret. Here's what you've been wantin'. Some snap beads. Thank you whoever gave us these things."

Rita interrupted with the confession, "I did. I do hope y'all will enjoy 'em. Mama let me pick 'em out myself."

"Right. Well, anyway thanks," Kat retorted.

I retrieved the beads and immediately strung them around my neck. "How do they look on me?" I asked Kat.

"All right, I guess if you like that sorta thing," she answered.

I grabbed the nearest gift and started removing the pink ribbon.

"I sure hope this is a deck of cards," Kat mumbled under her breath. "It's just gotta be."

"Yeah, a deck of cards would be great to share. I hope you are right," I said quietly.

Alas, it was a small box of pretend makeup.

"Oh my gosh! This is wonderful! Thank you so much, Teresa. How did you know that we wanted some? And look, some red fingernail polish to go with it," I said ecstatic. "Mama, can we open it now and put some on?"

"Not now," Kat said irritated. "Let's finish openin' up presents."

"Okay," I said and reached for the next gift to give to her. "It's your turn to open. Can't wait to see what's in this one. Aren't these the best birthday presents ever?" I sat the gift in front of Kat and said, "This one has only your name on it. What do you think it is?"

"I don't know. I'm not gonna guess any more. What do you think it is?" she asked quietly.

"Looks like one of those books of Life Savers," I said to Kat, trying to cheer her up.

To her surprise it was a book of Life Savers. Smiling for the first time since they started this routine, Kat gently placed the candy in her lap.

"Thank you, Mary and Midge," Kat said to the second set of twins in our grade.

The last gift had my name on it. As I read the card attached to it, I saw it was also from Mary and Midge. We had not realized that they brought two gifts, one for each of us.

Only another twin would know how important it is to get two presents, I thought as I slowly peeled away the paper to find a pair of two-inch plastic dress-up high heels, covered with pink feathers.

I squealed out, "Thank you. I love 'em!" And donned them immediately, giggling as I did.

I would have shared them with Kat, but I knew that she would never put them on her feet. The pink heels were definitely in my stack of gifts. What a wonderful birthday party it turned out to be. And it wasn't a complete washout for Kat. She got some Life Savers, and I was sure she would share them with me. Surely she wouldn't eat ten packs of Life Savers all by herself!

As we handed out the pinwheel party favors to each friend as they left, Kat apologized saying, "I wanted Mama to get red wax lips, but she got these instead. Sorry."

The last party guest to leave was Teresa. As we waited for her folks to arrive, we hop scotched our way down the dirt driveway. Kat clutched her book of Life Savers, having rescued it from the pile of gifts that were being pawed through by our siblings.

Teresa commented, "Kat, you sure do share good."

"Yeah, I guess I do. Why do you say that?"

"Well, you gave most of the birthday presents to Margaret and only kept the box of Life Savers. I share everything with my sister Kathryn. If I have two rolls of Life Savers, I always give her one. Are you gonna give Margaret half of the box?" Teresa asked.

Kat shrugged her shoulders, looked at Teresa quizzically, and responded quickly, "No, I've already given her everything else. The Life Savers are mine."

Not letting the subject rest, Teresa added, "What's your favorite flavor? I like the grape."

I butted in saying, "Oh, we both like the pineapple."

"Yep, the pineapple is my favorite," Kat agreed.

The next question caught Kat off guard when Teresa asked, "When are you gonna open up a pack? We could share right now. You're good at sharin'."

Kat peered down the driveway hoping to see the Ellises' car before saying, "Uhhh, sure. I'll give you the grape and I'll eat the pineapple. Margaret, what color do you want?"

"Guess I'll take the red one," I answered.

Kat blurted out, "Let's see who can suck it the longest. That person can have another one. Okay?"

That was Kat's way of sharing, hoping The Ellises would be here before she had to ante up another one.

Teresa took her turn at hop scotch commenting, "You're the best friend, Kat, sharing your only birthday present with us."

Pleased with the compliment, Kat got carried away and thrust the rest of the Life Saver roll into Teresa's hand saying, "Here, Teresa, you take the rest. You can share 'em with your sister."

After the guests had left, we cleaned up from the party. Kat and I gathered our presents and examined them again as we sat on the floor of our bedroom.

"I wanna share these gifts with you. I'm gonna let you have the makeup, snap beads, doll and doll clothes, diary, and those pink heels," Kat said as she shoved them toward me. Who gave us that diary anyway? Can't think of a more useless thing," Kat confessed.

Before I could answer her question, our six-year old sister, Kirk, opened the door and joined us on the floor.

"Kirk, we wanna share one of our presents with you," Kat said in a friendly tone. "Here you can have this diary and write your ABC's in it," she said as she snatched it from my stack and handed it to Kirk.

Tickled to get one of our gifts, Kirk jumped up and skipped out the door singing, "Happy birthday to me."

As Kirk exited, our four-year old brother, Allan, ran into the room asking, "Can I wear the pink high heels and put on the fingernail polish?"

"Sure," Kat said. "We will share 'em with you."

"But they're not yours to share. They were given to just me, remember?" I responded. "And, no you cannot play with 'em," I directed toward Allan. "But I'll polish your toenails after supper if you want me to."

As he left the room with an expectant look on his face, I turned to Kat and asked, "What do you think Mama and Daddy are gonna give us after supper tonight?"

"I don't know, but I hope it's not another diary. Maybe some new sandals so we don't have to wear those awful saddle oxfords all summer. What do you think?" Kat probed.

"Probably some clothes, or somethin' to wear. For sure not somethin' to play with," I responded.

After supper, the remainder of the birthday cake was placed on the table with ten candles.

Mama directed as she lit the candles for the second time today, "Margaret, you get to blow these out by yourself since Kat did earlier today. After we clear the table, we will give y'all your birthday presents."

"Do we hafta help clean the table since it's our birthday?" Kat asked, hoping for some kind of reprieve.

"Yes, you do. And the sooner it's cleaned, the sooner you get your presents," Mama said firmly.

When the kitchen was spick and span, we all gathered once again around the table where two presents rested.

Mama picked up a gift in each hand and presented one to each of us. My gift was long and thin and Kat's was in a square box. The gifts were wrapped in white tissue paper with red ribbon. But not for long, as we ripped into them as quickly as we could.

Written on the top of Kat's box was "Roy Rogers Gun and Holster Set." She wasn't going to fall for that one again.

"Is this really what it says it is or am I gonna find somethin' else inside? I thought I had a kickball at our party only to find some doll clothes in the box. Is it really a Roy Roger's gun and holster set? Or are y'all foolin' me?" Kat asked, leery of opening the box.

To her surprise, she found the number one item on her wish list! Within minutes the holster was hanging around her hips and she was practicing drawing and twirling. At the same time I was twirling my brand new baton, pretending to be the lead majorette in the high school band.

As our tenth birthday came to a close and we lay in our bunk beds, Kat on the top bunk, we whispered, "Happy birthday" to each other. I was cuddling with my brand new baby doll when a *pop* disturbed the silence. I realized that Kat was still playing with her new guns, trying to perfect her techniques.

In the years that followed, at Christmas, at birthday parties, or anytime gifts were present, upon opening a gift, Kat, being the dominant twin, made an instantaneous decision whether to keep it for herself or toss it into my reject stack. For instance, pogo sticks and hula hoops were Kat's and Kat's alone—no sharing. Whenever Kat received marbles, jacks, cards or pick-up sticks, she gladly shared them with me because she needed someone to play against. This was Kat's best opportunity for sharing—when it was convenient. I must admit, however, she didn't hesitate to share the Barbie doll, paper dolls and such with me.

GOIN' JAYBIRD

Kat, self-proclaimed leader of the posse, ran from around the corner of the house to the large picture window where Mama stood looking out at her brood of five. She yelled excitedly, "Mama! It's hot out here, can we go jaybird? Can we, Mama, can we? Bill and Allan are already jaybird." And in desperation added, "Please, can we, huh?"

Kirk and I chimed in begging, "Please, Mama, can we? Please! We wanna go jaybird, too. Why do Bill and Allan get to go jaybird and we don't? It's not fair!"

Summertime in Lafayette County, Mississippi, was the time of hot, dusty, sweaty days, and warm, breezeless, stagnant nights, when even breathing was an effort, sapping the life from our bodies. A favorite way to get around the oppressive heat was to go jaybird.

"Naked as a jaybird" was an expression we used to describe our attire or, more accurately, the lack of attire during the hot, dusty, dog days of summer. Sometime or another the term crept into our vocabulary, later shortened to "goin' jaybird" or simply "jaybird". Its origin is obscure, but more than likely is a Southern saying, since we have never heard it used outside the Deep South, but like so many other Southern sayings, seems evident. Anyway, it meant going naked, or in our neck of the woods, nearly naked, stripped to the waist and barefoot.

And we loved the freedom of not having sticky, sweaty clothes clinging to us during the hot, humid Mississippi summers. This was a freedom we looked forward to well before the end of school each spring. Jaybird days almost always began the first day of summer vacation. Another school year was over and we had the whole summer ahead with each day bringing both new and familiar adventures into our young lives. Shirts, socks and shoes came off, and the exhilaration of summer and expectation of doing nothing coursed through our bodies as we raced across the hills on our six-acre home place, our cares left behind.

This was our way of life every summer and, in our naiveté, we thought it would last forever. We, in our exuberance, never dreamed this carefree life would come to an end, and then without being aware that our lives were about to change, the good times, all too abruptly, ended. Puberty, like a sudden summer storm, came on us, hitting hard and hurtful. The King Twins faced reality with some startling news the first day of summer vacation 1958. That fateful day marked a turning point for us. We had turned ten years old only days before.

Jumping up and down that early overcast morning in late May in anticipation of going jaybird for the next three months, we anxiously awaited Mama's answer.

Not getting an immediate response to our nagging questions and assuming her silence meant approval, Kat yelled, "Take 'em off, girls!"

In one swift motion, three identical blouses that Mama had cut and sewn just days before were quickly unbuttoned and carelessly thrown in a heap on the ground.

Standing at the living room picture window watching the commotion and miming instructions, Mama's words met deaf ears as she pointed her bobbing index finger in our direction. Pretending not to understand her signing, we skipped off around the corner of the house—naked as jaybirds.

On the back patio we found Kat's cowboy gear haphazardly stacked on the picnic table. Known as the fastest gun in the neighborhood, Kat strapped her birthday present, a Roy Rogers' double gun and holster set, around her naked-as-a-jaybird waist. Slender hips struggled mightily to support the heavy guns as she mounted her trusty stick horse, Trigger. All that summer morning, Kat practiced drawing and twirling one of her new guns, while riding at break-neck speed around the backyard range. Drawing, firing, twirling and returning the gun to its holster, she polished her technique, achieving record time, comparable to any Saturday afternoon cowboy.

Kat's twirling routine would become a regular practice each morning as the five of us gathered on the back patio to plan the day's events. Well practiced with one gun, Kat proceeded to demonstrate to her posse of four how to rapidly draw both guns simultaneously, continuously twirling them around each index finger several times, and with skilled precision return them to their respective holsters. The posse, naked as jaybirds, encircled Kat, holding hands, jumping from one foot to another, laughing and cheering her on. With Roy Rogers and Gene Autry as our gun-slinging role models, we were confidant at that moment that Kat could outdraw even the singing cowboys.

At the end of her unbelievable demonstration, we were all eager to follow her into battle. My new birthday gifts, a doll named Sally and a baton, were lying on the ground at my feet. I knelt to retrieve them as Kat, throwing a leg over the back of our stick horse, carefully chosen days before as we strolled around the yard selecting the most suitable tree branch, rode by, swinging me on with one hand. We galloped off together to restore peace to the wild, unruly yard. Singing "Happy Trails To You" off-key in unison, the posse of five trotted toward the edge of the cliff, stopping abruptly at Kat's raised her hand, the signal to halt.

Dismounting, we tied our stick steeds to the nearest tree branch, dropped to our knees, then onto our bellies and crawled oh-so-quietly toward the edge of the cliff. With Kat in the lead giving directions to the deputies aligned four abreast behind her, we halted just short of the crest of the hill. Designated by Kat as the official scout, I received a silent signal from her to worm my way the remaining distance through knee-high weeds to peer over the edge. Clutching my doll and baton tightly to me, I found crawling on my elbows difficult. Growing impatient with my futile attempts to crawl, Kat snatched my cherished birthday presents from my fists and hurled them aside. Stunned that my new baby doll was cast aside so cruelly, I leapt to my feet and ran to rescue Sally. Touching her left index finger to her lips, Kat signaled me to be silent and resume my place on the ground with the remaining posse members, lest the rest of the neighborhood gang, in the enemy camp, would hear or see us. Snatching up the baton and Sally as quickly and quietly as possible, I crawled to my rightful place beside Kat, taking up my position once again as Scout.

Before I could complete the scouting mission, distant voices coming from the outer edges of our large back yard caught our attention, abruptly aborting my mission. Noticing that the enemy hadn't seen us, we silently crawled on our stomachs, formed a close circle with heads touching, to plot our attack. We knew the element of surprise was on our side.

Kat, leading the brigade, ordered each of us to take a strategic position encircling the enemy. Since Kat and I shared a horse, I would naturally have to ride into battle behind her. Stealth was the secret to capturing the bad guys. With everyone in place, Kat gave the signal by shooting her cap gun three times into the air. We charged our enemy, whooping and hollering at the top of our lungs, hoping to capture all of them. I fell by the wayside as Kat, in haste, galloped too fast for my legs to keep up. Glancing over her shoulder as she rode Trigger, Kat realized I had lost my grip from around her waist and made a spur-of-the-moment decision to backtrack to retrieve me. Remounting hurriedly, I struggled to protect baby Sally, clutching her tightly between the crook of my right arm and my naked-as-a-jaybird chest. The baton, held securely in the same hand as Sally, kept hitting my face as we galloped frantically away, while hanging on for dear life as I clutched Kat's waist with my free arm.

As our troops advanced, the enemy, disorganized by our sudden onslaught, scattered in all directions, leaving us alone in their camp facing each other. Breathless, we gathered on the back steps of our ranch-style brick home, while our horses enjoyed a well-deserved rest. With the horses leaning against the back of the house, the posse quickly gathered around the normal watering hole, grabbing the rubber hose, savoring the life-saving refreshment. Gasping for air, we took turns snatching the hose, greedily sucking in the cool clean water, drinking, restoring our energy.

Once our thirst was quenched, Kat began plotting another strategy for capturing our foes. But, before she could command us to our next posts, Mama opened the back door and handed out five paper cups, one for each member of the posse, with our names on them. Pleased to see our names scrawled across the outside of the cups, we knew this method of identification would prevent us from getting germs or cooties from our siblings. More importantly, we knew that in order to get more Kool-Aid at a later time, we each had to keep track of our own cup. Our cups were filled with chilled Kool-Aid. Thirsty, we quickly emptied them, guzzling the Kool-Aid faster than

Mama could pour. Sitting on the back steps naked-as-a-jaybirds with out-stretched arms toward the pitcher of Kool-Aid, we hoped it would never empty and when it did, each of us intended to be the lucky one getting the last drop.

At the time I couldn't quite put my finger on what was wrong, but as I started to drink, my eyes caught Mama looking at Kat and me, her mind seemingly preoccupied. In looking back, I now know she was considering how to tell us something that would change our lives. Mama started to speak, then, pausing as if to assure herself of what she wanted to say, cleared her throat, and began. What came next took us all by surprise, leaving us stunned.

Unbelieving and staring dumbfounded into Mama's eyes, Kat and I questioned in unison, "Ma'am? What did you say?"

Mama repeated what she had said, but this time with clarity word for word, "THE TWINS CAN NO LONGER GO WITHOUT A BLOUSE."

Bewildered by Mama's statement, Kat asked, "Does this mean we can't go jaybird anymore?"

Mama, not tolerating any sass, replied tersely, "Not only can you not go jaybird anymore, but you must begin wearing a training brassiere underneath your blouse."

Pausing momentarily, she patiently explained to us that we were growing up, becoming ladies and that, at our age, it wasn't lady-like to go without these intimate pieces of clothing. Blushing, Kat and I were uneasy that Mama would discuss this sort of sensitive subject in front of our sister and brothers. Even more distressing, was our Mama saying "brassiere," since no one, even within families, ever talked openly about such private and intimate things.

Wondering what kind of trouble we had gotten ourselves into, our siblings were all ears, paying special attention to the conversation as it unfolded between Mama and us. Abashed at hearing the words "brassiere," "our age" and "ladylike" all in the same sentence, we were stunned that these words described the situation in which we found ourselves.

Kat, the braver of us, desperately attempted to side track Mama, "What does our age have to do with it?"

I was wondering the same thing, but was afraid to ask. I knew we didn't need to wear one of those unmentionable things and was relieved that Kat had been the one to question. Mama pinned Kat with her eyes and gave the pat response, "Just because."

Those two simple words failed to satisfy, only adding to our confusion. Upset and angered by what we considered unfair treatment, the question in our minds was, *Why?*

The double standard hit hard, leaving us hurt and confused, making us more defiant. Why wasn't the same standard used for Kirk, Allan, and Bill? After all, Bill was not much older than us. It was just plain unfair—no two ways about it.

Standing firm, Mama answered again, "Just because," a slight smile touching her lips as she spoke, softening the response, seemingly sympathetic to our plight.

Bill gawked at us. He couldn't believe his good fortune. We could tell by the smirk now on his face that he was silently gloating on hearing our bad news. Nevertheless, we all stood, bunched in front of Mama, eyes wandering from one chest to another, looking for differences. Mouths agape and heads oscillating from chest to chest, Kat and I could only see likenesses, not differences. We didn't want to admit that there was a minute difference, but one so small that surely no one would notice. Comparing our chests to our siblings, we couldn't understand why a little puffiness was such a big deal. After all, there wasn't a black-eyed peas worth of difference between us and Bill—at least not that we could see as the five of us stood there staring. Why was there so much commotion over something so little? Why would something the size of a mosquito bite need training?

The most puzzling question to us was, *How and what was it going to train?* There was simply nothing there to train!

Exasperation showing on our faces despite our best efforts to conceal our feelings, Kat and I resigned ourselves to the fact that we were fighting a losing battle; past experiences had taught us that Mama always had the last word. The bottom line was we would wear blouses and training brassieres from that day forward, with no further questions asked.

Reluctantly following Mama's instructions, but knowing she had no choice, Kat unbuckled her gun and holster set and carefully placed them on the picnic table, with a stern look of warning that no one was to touch them. Gently I laid Sally and the baton beside Kat's valued possessions and glumly followed her up the back steps with Mama leading the way.

"Y'all better not bother our stuff while we're inside," Kat warned.

Looking over our shoulders, feet dragging as we shuffled up the steps, we saw Bill strapping on the guns, Kirk playing Mama to my Sally and Allan unsuccessfully trying his skills at twirling my baton. Kat started to turn and confront them, but remembering the determined look on Mama's face, shook her head, reconciled to our fate and disappeared through the doorway. A furtive glance exchanged between us, however, giving silent consent that they would pay—and would pay dearly.

We were furious that Kat's orders were so quickly disobeyed, and as Kat turned around to take corrective actions, Mama intervened, pointing her index finger toward the girls' bathroom directing, "Head down the hall, girls."

She shut the back door more forcefully than usual behind us, closing off all communications with our sister and brothers. Their snickering and laughing had taunted us, fueling our need for revenge. There was nothing we could do about them at the moment, but upon our return, they would get their just rewards for mocking us.

The powerful feeling of being free-riding cowgirls temporarily left behind, we slowly made our way side by side to the end of the long hallway to the girls' bathroom. With Mama walking one stride behind us, urging us on, we continued begging, hoping, that through some miracle, she would change her mind. At the end of the hallway the bathroom door loomed before us, and, sighing in defeat, we entered. Mama closed the bathroom door and handed us our recently discarded blouses and brand new training brassieres, telling us to put them on.

A wisp of a world-weary smile touched her lips as she gave us an ultimatum, "You girls can either stay in the bathroom all day and pout, or put these on and go out to play."

Unable to look her in the face, we stared hard-eyed at the blouses and training brassieres clutched in our white-knuckled fists, cruel representatives of our lost freedoms. Mama stared at us a moment longer then turned suddenly and left, closing the door firmly behind her. Disgusted, we threw the garments onto the bathroom floor and kicked them into the farthest corner, hoping they would, by that action, magically disappear.

Turning away, we were jerked back to reality by Kat's cap gun firing outside the bathroom window. Reacting to the intrusive sounds, we quickly climbed into the green bathtub, and on tiptoes, peered through the small-framed window. Stunned at what we saw, we fumed in silence. Kat banged on the window to get Kirk and the boys' attention. Furious, she raised both fists, shaking them threateningly at the former posse members.

Bill, showing off, raised both guns above his head, alternately firing them in the air. To my horror, Kirk was skipping around gleefully, holding Sally's hands, swinging her in a circle and singing, "Here We Go Round the Mulberry Bush." At the same time, Allan was marching, baton in hand, as if he were the drum major leading the school band in cadence.

Dejected by the spectacle, Kat hopped out of the tub, plopped onto the open toilet seat and cradled her head in her hands. With tears streaming unabated, I took a seat on the edge of the tub. Speechless, we sat dumbfounded, not knowing what to say, or do, or even how to comfort each other.

At last Kat stood and mumbled through clinched teeth, "They'll pay for this."

Once again, silence filled the room. Having studied our predicament in private meditation and seeing no other alternative, Kat ordered me, warning with her eyes not to argue, to gather the clothes for closer inspection. I handed Kat her brassiere. She looked at it with disgust, holding it at arm's length and dangling it by the shoulder strap between her index finger and thumb as if it were a smelly specimen in some science lab petri dish.

She stood there with the brassiere perched on the end of her finger and began twirling it around her trigger finger as she had done just minutes ago with her prized Roy Rogers gun. Obviously, the feel just wasn't the same as it slipped off her finger, sailed across the bathroom, and landed dangling across the open toilet. Lunging for it, Kat rescued the cursed thing just before it fell into the bowl. She held it up and, impishly, suggested it would make an excellent slingshot.

Stifling a smile at Kat's antics, I practiced hooking and unhooking the brassiere before attempting to put it on. It seemed easy enough, but I was leery of actually putting it on. I put my arms through the armholes, strapped the brassiere around my ribs and twisted my arms unnaturally behind my back. I desperately tried to insert the hook into the proper eye where the ends met between my shoulder blades. My shoulder sockets burned, in danger of becoming disjointed, as I fumbled clumsily to get the small hook into the even smaller eye. The short practice session ill-prepared me to actually put the contraption on. Minutes passed and my arms grew heavy. Collapsing on the toilet and pleading with my eyes, I stared at Kat and hoped she had noticed my struggles and would volunteer to fasten the thing for me. And, during all this time, she had made no attempt to put on her own brassiere.

Finally exasperated watching my struggles and with a mischievous smile, she blurted, "Turn around and let me fix it." I should have paid attention to that smile.

After assisting me, Kat began her own struggle and, from her grim look, I could tell she didn't want my help.

She snapped waspishly, "I can do this myself and better than you. I don't need your help. Just turn around and don't watch me!"

Turing away I faced the mirror and surreptitiously checked Kat's progress, or more aptly, her lack of progress. Seeming to take forever, Kat twisted and turned the training brassiere, first one way then the other, trying to figure it out. Frustrated at the brassiere, and even madder at the world, she finally realized hooking it first and then slipping it over her head might possibly work. With her head stuck in one of the armholes, Kat fussed and squirmed, elbowing me in the back several times, until the armhole stretched to the point that the brassiere shimmied down her scrawny body, past slender waist and hips.

As it sprawled around her feet, she stomped purposely out of it, kicked it aside with her left foot, and sighed audibly, relieved to be free of the awful contraption.

All the time I watched her mirrored image, fascinated at the unfolding scene, amazed that she was able to extract herself from the brassiere that had taken on a life of its own. Biting my lip to keep from giggling, and hesitant to give unwanted advice, I pretended not to notice. Kat inhaled deeply and studying the brassiere from several aspects, grudgingly gave it renewed respect. Determined not to let it beat her, she tried a different tactic. Wrapping it around her waist, she hooked it at her belly button. Pleased at finally finding a solution, she thrust her arms through the armholes and adjusted it, struggling to get the straps in place across her shoulders. Turning around she nudged me out of the way and with a glance in the mirror quickly slipped on her blouse and buttoned it.

Finished dressing, she glanced again in the mirror, then tapped me on the shoulder and growled, "Let's get outta here and get our stuff back."

Having completed the entire ordeal in less than thirty minutes, we bolted from the bathroom past Mama, our palms raised to push the screen door open, ready to play. But before we could cross the threshold, Mama, with a fresh pitcher of Kool-Aid in one hand, halted us dead in our tracks, insisting on a quick inspection of our attire.

With our blouses on and training brassiere straps now hanging down to our elbows, we stood silently while Mama looked us over. After a thorough once-over, she nodded approvingly, gesturing with her free hand that we could leave. Miserably, we moved toward the back steps, "in training," anxious to reclaim our birthday presents.

Wanting to see what transformation had taken place, Kirk, and Allan were perched on the picnic table eagerly awaiting our debut. Bill, looking at us strangely as if we were some sort of recently landed aliens, skipped around, lording over us; not exactly knowing why he had been spared, but pleased that he was still 'goin' jaybird.'

Forgetting revenge for the moment and ignoring the gawkers the best we could, Kat and I zeroed in on our valued possessions, which had been haphazardly dumped on the picnic table. Embarrassed at the unwanted attention she was getting, Kat grabbed her gun and holster set, strapping them on with more difficulty now that she was no longer jaybird. Confused at being changed from the rough and tumble Roy Rogers to the demur Dale Evans, Kat struggled briefly before getting the holster properly seated around her waist. Then she paused, glared at the boys and Kirk, and dared them to speak. They did not.

Dressed as Dale Evans, Kat felt deflated, yet still in control. She mounted her horse, now named Buttermilk after Dale's horse, and galloped off to find a secluded spot, leaving her troops behind. Abandoning Sally and my baton, and with heavy heart, I struggled to understand the fate that had so suddenly befAllan us. Catching up with Kat, the two of us raced downhill to the creek behind our house, hoping to lose those curious gawkers in our wake.

Tying Buttermilk at the water's edge, we splashed into the summer-warm creek water. With heads together we conspired how we could turn time back and once again run jaybird free. This was not a good way to begin our summer vacation, but with those finger-pointing siblings fast closing in on us, we could think of no reasonable solutions.

Angry at the world, Kat commented that at least we could still go barefoot, openly wondering if that would be the next freedom unceremoniously yanked from us. What did all of this mean? Did being "ladylike" imply having to wear shoes all the time? We studied our sunbaked feet in the shallow water, already summer tough, and decided surely they were safe from any and all other restraining devices. Like all changes that slip in when you least expect them, little did we realize on that summer day, that high heels would soon be pinching our feet.

As we waded in the warm stream, we privately considered our plight, all the time pulling and tugging at those tormenting training brassieres. The things didn't fit right and wouldn't stay in place as the straps slid off bony shoulders down to our elbows. We were constantly reaching inside our blouses, through the armholes, to pull the straps in place. No sooner were they adjusted than with the slightest movement would slip off again. Our roles reversed, we soon found that we were training the brassieres to stay in place, instead of them training us.

One moment they were binding and cutting and the next moment they were twisted under our armpits, chaffing and burning our skin.

The others followed us to the stream and asked all kinds of embarrassing questions. The most curious of all at age four, Allan tiptoed behind Kat and yanked her blouse up, exposing her brassiere.

Allan shouted for all to hear as he popped the elastic around her waist, asking, and little-boy curious, "What's that, Kat?"

Embarrassed, Kat slapped his innocent hands away, pushing him backward into the warm stream.

Kat gave Kirk and Bill orders, "Y'all take Allan back to the house and get him some dry clothes now."

We didn't want to be drawn into answering more of their silly questions. We wanted to be out of ear shot so we could talk in private. So while they were busy with Allan, we hurried away to find a secret hiding place – one so secluded that they could not spy on us.

The ridiculous questions they had fired our way so rapidly moments before were the same multitude of questions nagging at us now – ones that we needed to privately sort out. Paramount in our minds was, *What were we going to do about our mutual misery?*

Kirk and Bill moved away with Allan, occasionally glancing back at us over sunbaked shoulders. We hurried across the creek and headed for the old haunted house that faced our property. Here we hunkered down behind the tall bushes growing alongside the shabby dwelling, hiding from the others and the world, feeling betrayed by life. We sat alone, Indian style, a long time before either of us spoke. Careful words came first as we considered what to say. Then simultaneously we spilled our guts, expressing feelings neither of us had ever experienced before. I started to speak as a tear slid down my dirt-smeared cheek and the dam burst. I vented my frustrations with a barrage of questions. "Why did Mama do this to us? Do you really think we gotta wear these things every day? If we gotta wear 'em, why doesn't Kirk have to? And how will we ever learn to put 'em on?"

Kat, frustrated as well, kept repeating, "I don't know," after each question.

We lay back, watching a wispy cloud sailing by overhead. Ashamed at revealing our most private thoughts, Kat complained about her training brassiere. She unbuckled the gun and holster at her waist before jerking her miss-buttoned blouse off to fix what was wrong. Her mistake was she had hooked it in the front and left it there. To my horror, the cups were training the shoulder blades at her back. Doubling over with laughter at the sight got me a squint-eyed look from Kat as she removed her arms from the straps, twisting the brassiere into its proper position.

As she forced her arms into the armholes, I angered her even more by saying, "That's what you get for not lettin' me help you put it on."

Kat blurted, "Well, yours isn't on right either."

Wondering what she meant, I twisted around trying to see what was wrong. Unbuttoning and removing my blouse, I reached around my back only to find that the back strap was grossly tangled. Unknown to me, she had purposely twisted the back strap around three times before hooking it. Feeling betrayed, I unhooked it, straightened out the strap, and re-hooked it from the front as Kat had done. With brassieres properly positioned and our blouses re-buttoned, we sat on the ground alternately laughing and crying about what fate and Mama had dealt us. We still couldn't figure out what we were going to do to change things.

We were hot and sweaty and constantly adjusting those aggravating undergarments, but with time, we adjusted to our new harnesses. Kat reasoned that, under the circumstances, with no one else around, it would be okay to go jaybird just one last time. Convincing me to go along with her suggestion was relatively easy. I guess I was a bit hesitant to toss clothes aside, but being acutely uncomfortable, I sided with Kat's reasoning.

We quickly disrobed and examined with renewed interest the garments that were to be a part of our daily routine. We noticed that a part of the strap would lengthen then shorten when pulled in the opposite direction. Pulling the straps to the shortest length, I tried mine on, and much to my amazement, the small training cups were tucked under my neck, choking me. At the same time, Kat was pulling the straps to the longest length and found the brassiere dangling below her ribs. Somewhere in between, we realized, was the right length for our bodies, but then tiring of the game, we laughingly tossed our brassieres and our blouses on nearby bushes.

Enjoying the breeze at our backs, we climbed trees and played hopscotch, cares forgotten. We were children reveling in this, our last hurrah, well aware that our childhood had ended abruptly this morning when Mama handed us those brassieres and told us to put on our blouses. Saddened at childhood lost, we turned to each other for muted comfort, sympathy, and support. At that moment, we formed a relationship that would strengthen as we grew into womanhood. We were secure in knowing that no one could take this bond away from us, each knowing how the other one felt at this vulnerable time. We had, we realized, thought and acted as one in a time of distress.

We basked in the sunshine. As time fled by, we didn't realize that our skin was getting blistered in the overcast morning light. A racket in the nearby bushes where we had tossed our blouses and brassieres brought us quickly back to reality. Startled, we jumped up from our hiding place in time to see Bill racing away, holding our blouses and brassieres like banners fluttering in the wind as he sprinted toward the house yelling for Kirk and Allan to look at his trophies.

Even though Bill had a sizable head start, Kat snatched up her holster set and we ran after him, closing in with every stride. Approaching the creek, he stopped to size up the width, and with us quickly gaining on him, misjudged his ability to jump across it. Glancing over his shoulder at two annoyed sisters almost on him, he launched his flailing body out over the water. Landing well short of the far bank, he surfaced and slogged out of the creek and scrambled up the other side. Soaking wet, he slowed down. Waving our dripping garments in front of him, he was slowed even more with the wet clothes slapping him in the face. In contrast to his self-imposed handicaps, our natural athletic abilities gave us clear advantage over him. As we had done many times before, we easily jumped the creek, and quickly overtook the soaked mischief-maker. When Bill was less than ten yards from the back door and safety, Kat lunged and tackled him at the ankles. Bringing him down hard, she silenced him for the moment.

Straddling his back and pinning him to the ground, she yelled, "Grab 'em, Margaret, and run to our favorite hidin' place. I'll be right behind you. I've just gotta teach him a lesson."

Anxiously jumping from foot to foot, I was watching and waiting for a break in the fight so I could yank the clothes from Bill's grasp and take off.

Frustrated, I fired back at Kat, "I can't get 'em. He won't let go. Help me get his fingers open."

Kat responded, huffing and puffing, "I can't. I'm holdin' him down. You gotta get 'em."

Kirk and Allan were sitting on the picnic table, watching the action unfold. Kirk was cradling Sally and Allan was pitching the baton in the air. Both were giggling, enjoying the entertainment from the safety of distance. Bill and I were in a tug-of-war over the clothes. At the first opportune moment, I attempted to jerk both sets of garments out of Bill's fists. Kat struggled to keep him still so I could get our clothes released, but his tight grip wouldn't loosen. Finally prying his fingers apart, I pulled to yank the clothes free. The sound of material ripping stopped us dead in our tracks. Realizing what had happened, Bill and Kat scrambled to their feet and Bill tossed the garments at me, renouncing any and all responsibility for the torn blouse.

Stunned, we looked up to see Mama standing inside the back door watching and waiting, tapping her foot impatiently for us to finish fighting. Tiring of the shenanigans, she slammed the back door as she hurried out to investigate the ruckus. I quickly hid the ripped clothes behind my back, praying Mama would not notice what we had done.

Easing backward to the picnic table, I discarded the garments before Mama could get her hands on them. Once again we stood rigidly before Mama on the patio, naked as jaybirds, as we had been just hours before. Mama turned to Bill for answers. He, of course, blabbed everything we had done from the time we left the house. With his tell-all running account, we realized that Bill had been spying on us the entire time. Looking at us to confirm or deny Bill's story, Mama pinned us with her eyes and questioned us further to get at the truth. At that exact moment, all attention was diverted to Kirk and Allan, who, by then, were atop the picnic table examining our discarded brassieres.

Allan was busy strapping on one of the training brassieres and Kirk was fastening it, just as he jumped down with baton in hand to march to the beat of his own rhythm, "Hup, two, three, four," over and over again.

Capturing everyone's attention, he strode off down the hill with Kirk in tow. As our laughter subsided, we knew our punishment would bring on a drastic change: we would have to wear training brassieres every day for the rest of our lives, starting today, even over our sunburned skin. We moaned, but knew that was the last word on the subject. We had been accused, judged and sentenced, and now court was adjourned. Our only consolation was in the satisfaction of knowing that Kat had won the fight with Bill. Gloating, smiling and jaybird, he strutted away knowing he was the real winner.

That day, and everyday thereafter, punishment was routinely meted out. Kat and I helped each other get into the cursed training brassieres, mumbling under our breaths at the unfairness of life and wondering if we would ever be able to put the things on by ourselves. The whole process was just too complicated, unnatural and awkward! *How did other girls put them on by themselves,* we mused, but at least we had each other.

We lost a sacred freedom that fateful summer – just one of many we'd lose as puberty approached and we grew older. To become ladies would not be easy, especially if we couldn't go jaybird ever again. Little did we know that training brassieres were only the beginning of the trials and tribulations associated with growing up – becoming ladies.

NEILSON'S ON THE SQUARE

The closing of summer in 1959 caught Mama busy at the sewing machine. She was putting the finishing touches on the last of the jumpers, blouses, skirts and dresses that would become our fall wardrobe.

A few weeks prior to sewing on the final buttons, Mama took me aside after breakfast and stated, "After lunch I want you to put on your Sunday dress and shoes and accompany me to Neilson's Department Store to help find some new patterns and cloth. I need to begin sewing your outfits right away if I'm going to have them ready for the new school year."

"Can Kat go, too?" I asked hoping we could collaborate on the final selections.

"No. Not this time. I trust your judgment. Katherine will adjust to whatever we pick out," Mama said confidently.

"Oh. Yes, Ma'am. She will. I can't wait to look at the pretty materials. Can I pick out the dress patterns? And the materials?" I asked, thrilled that Mama wanted my help.

"We'll work together in selecting both," Mama said, smiling at me.

I scurried out the back door as quickly as I could to find Kat to tell her about my good fortune. I glanced around and finally located her at the top of the tallest tree near the back of the yard. She was gazing off over the top of the house and humming a silly little tune, all in a world of her own. I shouted, "Come down. I gotta tell you somethin' important."

"What is it?" she yelled, frowning for having her solitude interrupted.

"I'm goin' with Mama to Neilson's this afternoon to pick out patterns and material for our new school outfits," I shouted in reply.

"Okay. I'll be right down to get ready to go, too," Kat replied.

"No. Mama just wants me to go this time," I yelled back.

But Kat was quickly retreating from the top branch, retracing the familiar path that took her to the highest point. She made her final swing and jumped from a limb some three feet high on the tree. Landing on her feet, she asked out of breath, "Why can't I go?"

"I don't know why. It's probably 'cause I helped clean the breakfast dishes and you ran out the back door as soon as you finished your last bite," I said, still peeved at her for abandoning me earlier that morning.

"Well, she doesn't want me in that ol' kitchen. Says me being left-handed makes me break dishes and stuff," Kat retorted.

"Anyway, Mama said I can pick out the patterns and materials for both of us," I explained.

"You gonna get some of that material that's made out of checkers?" she asked. "You know that checkered one we saw a while back when we were in Neilson's."

Momentarily confused I asked, "Checkers, what checkers?" Then it dawned on me what she meant. "Oh, you mean the plaid material. Yeah, I liked that, too."

"Just don't get any pink or purple material," Kat pleaded.

"I wouldn't get those colors 'cause they are spring colors, not fall. Don't you know anything about clothes?" I admonished.

"Okay. Okay. Do you want to climb the tree or go to the creek 'til Mama calls us for lunch?" Kat asked, eager to change the subject.

"No, I don't wanna get dirty. I'm going inside to get ready to go to Neilson's," I replied.

I watched Kat climb back to her perch at the top of the tree, then skipped off toward the house humming mindlessly.

Weeks later, Mama now had most of the fall outfits sewn, ironed, and hanging in our closets. Mama handed me the final blouse saying, "Hang this with the plaid jumper. Tomorrow morning I'll have a surprise for all of you. Now run along and get your bath. Remind Katherine to brush her teeth and make sure she takes her bath. Y'all get ready for bed."

"Yes Ma'am. I will," I said as I ran to give Mama's messages to Kat.

Mama's firm voice shook us awake early the next morning, the last day of summer vacation. I awoke to a hot, muggy September morning with my pleasant dreams of lolling around all day doing nothing but living interrupted. Her sharp voice commanded, "Hop up, girls, get dressed and be at the breakfast table in fifteen minutes. After breakfast we're going to Neilson's to buy new school shoes."

I rolled over in bed to face Mama. Bleary eyed, I found an empty portal and wondered if the words I heard were real or merely a part of my dream. Footsteps receded down the hall as the impact of her instructions hit me. Mama repeated the demands twice more at my other siblings' doorways on her way to the kitchen. I hastily rolled out of the lower bunk and landed face down on the hardwood floor, remembering Mama's promise of a surprise.

Jumping up, I shook Kat awake. "We're goin' to Neilson's after breakfast. Wake up, Kat. We're gonna get some new shoes!" Good news indeed.

Kat forced an eye open and stared at me contemptuously. Her dazed look told me she hadn't heard a word so I repeated the good news. I grabbed the sheet and pillow that now covered Kat's head. She bolted from the top bunk, landing on both feet to face me, the importance of this day finally dawning on her.

Quickly throwing on identical plaid dresses, we found clean socks to wear and searched for last year's old saddle oxfords we hadn't worn since school ended last May. Saddle oxfords were day-in-and-day-out-shoes for nine long months during the school session. They were made of leather and were uncannily similar to combat boots. The heavy duty, black and white boat-like shoes could take the immense punishment meted out by us and we hated them.

Kat looked under the bunk bed while I searched the closet floor. Throwing aside a summer's collection of jump ropes, jacks, skates, pop-beads, paper dolls, dolls, and doll clothes, I finally spied one shoe that was mine and yelled, "I found one of mine!"

I freed it from the pile and threw it over my shoulder into our bedroom where it bounced off Kat's right arm. Pushing me aside in her hurried quest to find her shoes, Kat squeezed into the small closet, squirmed to the far corner and began flinging everything in her path. Dodging the flying objects, I crawled to the other corner and together we methodically searched for the missing shoes.

Kat came out with a pair, claiming, "Here's mine!"

But on closer inspection one shoe proved to be mine. I grabbed for it. Kat yanked it away and sat haughtily on the floor, shoving her feet into both scruffy shoes at the same time. Since her feet were a half size bigger than mine, she soon realized the left shoe didn't fit and, piqued, tossed it my way.

I had not realized my feet had also grown. It was difficult for me to cram my feet into worn-out shoes that were now far too small. Lacing them up loosely, I joined Kat in the hunt for her lost shoe with only minutes to spare before Mama would be calling us again to the breakfast table. Panic registered on Kat's face. We crawled to our built-in cabinets and started tossing out toys and outgrown clothes in a desperate attempt to find the missing shoe. Almost ready to give up the search and face Mama's frown, Kat found it in the back of the last cabinet.

Hopping clumsily on one foot, she managed to shove her foot into the lace-less shoe. "Are you sure you've got the right shoes on? These are way too small for me," Kat complained.

On cue, Mama called us to breakfast. We rushed toward our door, but turned back to gape horrified at the mess we had created. Hastily we threw everything back into the cabinets and closet and raced for the kitchen. When we got there, Kat, as was her usual habit, directed, "Get the napkins and forks and set the table."

Striding importantly past Mama, she plopped herself in her assigned chair, waiting for service. I counted out forks and napkins to properly set the table. Kat grabbed a set from my hands and tossed them haphazardly onto her breakfast mat, impatient for Mama to dish up the grub. Having completed the task of setting the table, I took my place between Bill and Kat and waited for breakfast to be doled out.

Once seated, I leaned over and whispered in Kat's direction, "I don't want another pair of saddle oxfords this year. What do you want?"

"I want some white tennie shoes so I can run faster," she replied, a satisfied look in her eyes. "What about you?"

"I wanna pair of patent-leather shoes for dress up. Rita has a pair and they're so pretty. I want some just like hers," I responded quickly.

"Dress up? Why do you want dress up? You crazy or somethin'? You can't play hopscotch and marbles or run in those kinda shoes. Playin' outside is lots more fun than dressin' up. You'll get tennie shoes if I have anything to do with it," Kat threatened emphatically.

Before I could respond, Mama turned from the stove with breakfast in hand, temporarily halting all conversation. Finishing the meal in record time, we silently hoped that this might be the year to get the shoes that we each fancied. Then, with kitchen and grooming chores complete and eager to get to Neilson's Department Store as quickly as possible, all five siblings raced for the car's prized front seat, as Mama completed the task of locking the house. Getting to the car first, Kat jumped into the shotgun position of the four-door sedan and slammed the door as an unyielding affirmation to the rest of us that she would ride in the coveted seat.

Tired of listening to us argue over who would sit where, Mama silenced her fighting brood, relocating Kat to the least desirable place in the middle of the back seat. Bill oozed smugness as he sat in the place of prominence, replacing Kat in the front. Kirk and I occupied the bookend-window seats, leaving Allan to sit between Bill and Mama in the front. With Mama now in control of the situation, Kat, feeling the futility of fussing about the seating arrangement, put up little resistance as we journeyed to town to make the annual purchases.

As we drove, Kat and I argued in whispers about the kind of shoes we wanted. She insisted that we should get tennis shoes. I shook my head vigorously from side to side to let her know I wanted dressier shoes.

She whispered tight lipped, "You just wait and see!"

Mama pulled to the curb at Neilson's, and with a no-nonsense look on her face, turned and pointed a bobbing finger at each of us. Then with a stern tone in her voice began the litany of dos and don'ts, "No fighting, don't touch anything, be polite, keep quiet unless spoken to, say yes, Ma'am, no, Ma'am, yes, Sir and no, Sir, and be on your best behavior. Each of you look at me. Look me in my eyes and tell me you understand my instructions. You are to mind your manners," she added as an afterthought.

In turn, we each responded affirmatively, but I noticed that Kat's response was little more than a grunt as she was trying to avoid looking at Mama eye-to-eye.

Pausing at Kat, Mama made a few more don'ts adding to her list, "Don't pick a fight with Margaret or Bill, don't touch anyone, and absolutely no running. Do you understand me?"

A soft barely audible, "Yes, Ma'am," was Kat's meek reply.

"Now, go to the door, line up and wait for me," Mama directed.

Acknowledging all of Mama's directions, five bobbing heads nodded in unison as we rushed from the car. We quickly lined up at Neilson's front door in single file behind our youngest brother, Allan, and waited for Mama to join us. Holding the door open, Mama greeted each of us with a final silent warning as each of us stepped over the threshold. We marched like little soldiers through the smells of new clothes to the back of the store in our old battered shoes. As we filed past several bolts of material, the bright patterns caught our attention. With temptation in the path, Kat fingered the shiny red-checked cloth and whispered at my back, "Why didn't you get some of this pretty material?"

I reached out to follow her lead but had second thoughts when I saw Mama striding purposefully toward us.

Whispering anxiously, "Let's go, Mama's comin'." I pulled Kat along by the arm.

Mama intervened and pointing to a chair in the shoe department said emphatically, "Sit. Don't move an inch and don't touch or say another thing. Do you understand me?" That 'do you understand me' was Mama's favorite expression.

Without answering, we sat stiff-backed in the row of chairs, from youngest to oldest. We held on to the hope of starting the school year in our dream shoes – anything but Buster Brown saddle oxfords. Five pair of smelly, well-worn shoes followed by five pair of equally smelly socks were soon scattered across Neilson's shoe department floor as each waited, anticipating our turn with the salesman who would measure our bony feet. With measurements taken, we each retrieved our socks and donned them once again. The salesman had a brief conversation with Mama and abruptly disappeared behind a curtain. This caught our younger brother, Allan's attention. At just five years old, he was curious to know what lay behind the parted partition. He hopped down from his chair and scampered in pursuit, quickly covering the space between his seat and the still swaying curtains and vanished before our eyes.

Startled at Allan's retreat, Kat shouted, "Oh no! Stop! Allan, you can't go through there." She leapt to her feet and hurried after him. When she caught up with him, she bear-hugged him into submission, then hauled him, kicking and screaming, back to his chair.

Before Mama could reprimand either of them, the salesman reappeared with ten shoeboxes, five stacked on each arm. He looked like an acrobat artist at the circus trying to balance all those boxes. Two boxes were placed in front of each chair. One of each of our boxes was labeled Buster Brown. Simultaneously, Kat and I reached to open the box not labeled Buster Brown.

When I opened mine I was exhilarated to find a pair of shiny black patent leather shoes for dancing and dress up. Kat eyed my shoes and groaning in misery lost all hope of owning a pair of white tennis shoes. Frowning, she reluctantly dragged out identical matches to my black patent leathers and Buster Brown saddle oxfords. The salesman slid our feet into the patent shoes first to make sure they fit properly, then the Buster Browns. Once the Buster Browns were laced and tied tightly, he placed the old pair into the empty Buster Brown shoe box.

With elbows on her knees and head cradled in spread hands, Kat muttered, "I hate these ol' shoes. I'll be glad when I grow up and can buy my own. I can't run fast in these awful things!" Through separated fingers, Kat found herself staring at Mama's feet. Jerking her head up startled, she prayed that Mama hadn't heard her complaints.

Understanding her daughter's disappointment, Mama patted her back explaining, "When you kick rocks, this is all you can expect to get. You're just too tough on shoes. Now, you can wear your new saddle oxfords home and start breaking them in. And try not to scuff them up before school starts tomorrow."

Mama retreated to pay for the shoes as I turned, gloating to Kat, and whispered, "At least we got dress-up shoes, so I guess you can play dress up with me."

Irritated at hearing this, Kat spouted angrily, "Never! Not in a million years!"

Mama appeared abruptly and, tucking the receipt into her purse, studied us for a moment. Silencing us with a slight shake of her head, she handed each of us our two boxes of shoes and, without a word, directed us to the car.

A day that started out on a high note now found us leaving the store deflated. Now we began the painful task of breaking in our new saddle oxfords. Buying the new shoes one size larger, Mama hoped the sturdier leather shoes, unlike tennis shoes, would last an entire school year. We slowly dragged ourselves through the store, exaggerating the simple task of putting one new shoe in front of the other. Leading the pack to the exit, Bill tripped and fell over his own feet. With long spidery legs extended, Bill brought down Kat, then me like dominos. Boxes and shoes went flying in all directions. Bill, Kat and I lay sprawled in a heap on the floor of Neilson's Department Store, pushing and shoving in an effort to get up. Everyone was staring at us. Embarrassed, I jumped up, smoothed my dress, and gathered my scattered shoes and boxes, leaving Kat and Bill struggling to regain their composure. With a hint of a smile at the corners of her mouth, Mama quickly intervened, realigning us on our journey to the car. With renewed focus on the new shoes already hurting our aching feet, we struggled to walk a straight line.

"My shoes are too big and I can't walk right," Kat complained as she walked backward facing me. "I can't believe we got the same ol' shoes as last year!"

Later we adapted to the oversized shoes by wearing two pairs of bobbie socks to take up the wiggle room. For the first few weeks walking in those new shoes was awkward and to this day, the bony knots on our heels give testament to the abuse our feet endured.

THE OLD SWITCHEROO

The sixth grade was one of the toughest and most chAllanging times in our young lives. Many factors contributed to the difficulties we faced – socially and academically. Puberty was changing every aspect of our awkward physical appearance. Then we learned that we were enrolled in the school's most dreaded teacher's class. As we saw it, our only salvation was that we were going to be able to tackle this problem together. There had been talk of placing us in separate classes, but remembering the anxious moments of being separated in first grade, we begged to be together. Every year afterward, we pleaded to be placed together at the beginning of school and got our wish, year after year. However, this year we didn't expect to ever end up in Mrs. Stern's sixth grade classroom. Tough? Yes indeed!

A chAllange loomed before us, but it was hardly fair – two against one. This was the first time we fully realized we could utilize the many advantages of being identical twins. This was the year that we began to put into practice the art of switching places and identities. And, with a little practice, we perfected the art of impersonation.

It came naturally to us, especially when backed into a corner.

As much as we dreaded having Mrs. Stern for a teacher, she was even less enthusiastic about having us as students. We couldn't quite understand why she seemed to take an immediate dislike to us. Could it be she just didn't want two of the same person in her classroom, or did our reputations precede us? She seemed to struggle daily with Which is Which as we constantly kept her confused and guessing. Dressed as we always did in identical clothes, every day posed a further threat to her ability to control the entire class. We knew Mrs. Stern was frustrated with her lack of confidence in being able to correctly identify us. We were determined that we were not going to give her the satisfaction of telling us apart – even when she guessed correctly. Many times she knew she had called on the correct twin, but she couldn't prove it, and we weren't about to tell her differently. In addition, she didn't get any help from our classmates because... well, most of them couldn't to tell us apart either. We must have been her worst nightmare!

Each morning Mrs. Stern would greet us as we crossed the threshold into her domain saying sweetly, "Good morning, Katherine. Good morning, Margaret," looking at us directly as she called our names.

I would say, "Mornin', Mrs. Stern. I'm Margaret."

And Margaret followed with, "Good Mornin' Mrs. Stern. I'm Katherine."

As we sidled past her toward the middle aisle to find our seats, Margaret whispered, "She still thinks I'm you."

Gleefully, I responded, "I think we can do this switchin' thing all year long, don't you?"

Margaret nodded in agreement and together we smiled broadly as we found our desks and took a seat, ready for the day's lessons to begin. And so, Mrs. Stern's struggles continued as we played the game of The Old Switcheroo, day in and day out.

Seating us alphabetically seemed the easiest way for Mrs. Stern to tell us apart. This classification strategy helped us to implement our own plan – switching desks. As a matter of fact, it added considerably to our cause. Little did she know that by alphabetizing, she gave us the perfect setup, as the seating arrangement worked to our advantage.

On the first day of sixth grade we stood with our classmates in a semi-circle in the front of the classroom waiting for assigned seats. We fidgeted nervously waiting for desk designations. No one wanted to be in the dreaded front row seats!

Our luck held as Mrs. Stern called, "You twins take your places. Margaret, you're in the last seat, and Katherine, you take the seat in front of her."

Eyeballing us as we passed by her desk, Mrs. Stern commanded, "Stop just a minute and let me look at you two. Let me see how I can tell you apart."

Staring at us to identify differences and finding none, she asked, "Is there any way to tell you two apart?"

We looked into each other's face at our mirror image and weighed our options. A slight smile touched Margaret's lips as we silently dismissed the possibility of giving her a hint. Elbow nudging me to answer Mrs. Stern's question, Margaret bowed her head meekly, abandoning all eye contact with the instructor.

Jerking my head up, I faced our teacher and managed to eyeball her. Then with an overly-sweet tone, I whispered barely audible, "No, Ma'am. Nobody can tell us apart. Sometimes not even Mama."

Of course, our close friends could tell us apart, but we really didn't want Mrs. Stern to know that, and as we walked confidently down the middle aisle together, I took my 'rightful' place at Margaret's desk, leaving her no choice but to sit in mine.

No reason for Mrs. Stern to get the upper hand right off, I thought.

Unknown to our teacher, we sat at each other's desk almost every day and many times we switched when we returned from recess. More times than not, whichever one of us entered the aisle first had the choice of which desk to sit in, a constant fruit basket turn over.

"Oh, well," I confessed on many occasions. "It's lots of fun to keep her guessin'."

Switching desks often meant we routinely submitted in-class assignments with each other's name on them. The fact that I was left-handed and Margaret was right-handed never posed a problem as one might think since we practiced daily writing exactly alike. As Mrs. Stern patrolled the aisles we were prepared to switch writing hands when necessary, and so we were confident we had all the bases covered.

A few weeks into the fall term found us implementing another shenanigan. As September turned into October, in-class arithmetic assignments became more and more difficult. Margaret struggled to get her work done on time so we began the second phase of The Old Switcheroo. Being fairly proficient in arithmetic, I could finish both of our worksheets by the time most of our classmates could complete theirs. The only hitch in our scheme was that Mrs. Stern constantly walked the aisles checking each student's progress. She particularly kept an eagle eye on us, ensuring we were doing our own work. While Margaret was squirming nervously at her desk and struggling to look busy, I was quickly finishing the same assignment. Once I completed my worksheet, timing became a critical factor as we waited for Mrs. Stern to stroll past our desks. Once her back was to us, we quickly switched papers and I hurriedly completed Margaret's twenty problems of adding mixed fractions. Before time was called, we each sat proudly holding our own work.

Getting everyone's attention, Mrs. Stern instructed, "Students in rows one and two swap papers across the aisle. Rows three and four do the same as well as those of you in five and six. When I have finished calling out all the answers put the grade at the top of the sheet. Each problem counts off five points if missed. After you have put the correct score on the paper, you will then return it."

I usually made a better grade than Margaret since I purposefully missed a problem or two on her sheet. This ploy was used to avoid making Mrs. Stern suspicious.

But if she should suspect something was amiss, we were confident that she couldn't prove any foul play on our part.

On this particular day, Margaret made an 80 and I made a 90. That seemed pretty fair to me, but not to Margaret as she poked me in the back when she saw her grade.

When the lunch bell rang I stood in line ahead of Margaret waiting to go to the cafeteria. In a low irritated voice she asked, "How come you always make better than me? It's not fair."

I retorted more curtly than needed, "Well, I do all the problems. Anyway, I didn't have time to check over the ones you worked yourself. So those are the ones you probably missed."

Margaret, on the other hand, was more proficient in reading assignments and often had to come to my rescue. Mrs. Stern routinely called on students to read passages from the social studies book – passages that were homework assignments from the night before. I never read the social studies homework because I hated to read and memorize facts. Margaret completed all the assignments in this subject by answering homework questions at the end of each chapter. Once her work was completed, we had to consider the problem of re-wording the answers. Margaret was also real good at re-wording. To sum it up, we had a good deal going. Margaret did the social studies homework and I did the arithmetic homework.

Never being prepared for in-class reading assignments, I took my chances that if called upon Margaret would bail me out. Sometimes switching places didn't work out very well. Unfortunately for me, we had switched desks after lunch on this particular day with Margaret in the seat in front of me.

As social studies class began, Mrs. Stern announced, "I want row three to begin reading chapter five to the rest of the class."

I quickly deduced that I would be reading paragraph six. I whispered nervously to Margaret, "Look what I have to read. It's the longest paragraph in the lesson. What am I gonna do? I can't read all of that stuff out loud, and then she's gonna ask me a bunch of questions I can't answer. What am I gonna do?"

Barely shaking her head, she indicated that no help could come from her.

In a panic, I sat back in my seat and silently began reading to myself those words that I would have to repeat to my classmates in just a matter of minutes. Reading aloud made me extremely on edge to such a degree that I couldn't comprehend what I had just read for worrying about pronouncing each word correctly. And to complicate matters further, Mrs. Stern always questioned the reader on comprehension of the text.

I fidgeted and fretted, which I didn't do often. It was my turn to squirm. I knew Margaret felt my anxiety and knew there was little she could do to help me. To make matters worse, Margaret was worried about getting a bad grade since I would be reading and answering for her. As I slowly read silently to myself, it seemed that the first four readers sped through their reading assignments, and

I hadn't even read through my entire paragraph once. Panic surged through me as Margaret began to read. She had the shortest paragraph so I knew it wouldn't be long until I had to perform as her. Margaret, reading as me, deliberately recited slowly and elaborated on the questions asked by Mrs. Stern, who was visibly surprised that I/Margaret had answered the questions correctly. After praising me/Margaret for my knowledge of the subject matter, Mrs. Stern looked at desk six and called upon Margaret/me to read the next paragraph.

Margaret, holding her breath, was hoping and praying that I would perform adequately and as eloquently as she had just done for me. Nervous and jittery, legs shaking, I opened my mouth to read the first word, and as I did, was saved by the recess bell ringing. That wonderful sound saved me. Relief washed over my face and Margaret slowly let her breath out. I knew then that her silent prayer had just been answered.

Turning to face me, Margaret mouthed, "Saved by the bell."

Before dismissing the class for recess Mrs. Stern announced, "We'll finish this reading assignment when we return." My mouth fell open when it dawned on me that I had just been rescued.

We simultaneously slammed our books shut, raced onto the playground and ran as fast as we could go to the ditch behind the swings. Sitting Indian style on the ground at the far end of the playground we finally caught our breaths.

I looked directly into Margaret's eyes and gasping between words blurted, "We just pulled it off. Can you believe it?"

Margaret rebutted, "No, we didn't pull anything off. The bell saved you."

"Well, it saved you, too, 'cause I was readin' for you. When we go back in, you sit in your own desk so you can read for yourself and you'll get a good grade. I don't like readin' that old stuff so you can just do it and lots better than me," I explained.

We both started giggling then realized precious recess minutes were being wasted on talking.

Not wanting to squander the entire recess on academic matters, I jumped up and skipped off yelling over my shoulder to Margaret, "Come on. Let's play kickball with the boys."

This problem was now resolved in my eyes, and I left Margaret standing alone to deal with the remaining details. When recess ended, we quietly entered the classroom. Margaret strolled down the middle aisle confidently claiming her rightful seat in desk six. Following in her footsteps, I was pleased with the way the events had unfolded. I sat proudly in desk five, knowing that I was completely off the hook and had a great grade in Mrs. Stern's grade book thanks to my twin. As Margaret finished reading and answering the questions it was evident she had also received a good grade, well deserved for both performances.

One day during the school term our school-day pictures arrived. At 2:45 that afternoon Mrs. Stern stopped our regular class activities to distribute the pictures. As she sat behind her desk looking at the sets of photos, Mrs. Stern called each student to come to her desk to receive their packet. When she picked up one of our packets, she called for one of "The King Twins" to come to her desk to identify which set belonged to each of us. Neither of us wanted to come forward. We sat in the back of the room arguing in a soft whisper, trying to decide which one of us would take the dreaded trip.

She held the packet of pictures up for everyone to view. Neither of us got up. Exasperated, Mrs. Stern finally called, "Katherine, come up here immediately and identify these pictures."

Since I was sitting in my correct desk, I had no choice but to go. Intimidated by Mrs. Stern's agitated voice, I shuffled pigeon-toed, slowly to the front of the classroom. To my horror and her aggravation, I couldn't identify whether the pictures were of me or Margaret. I stared at the package, dumbfounded that I couldn't find a way to tell Mrs. Stern the horrible truth of not knowing which twin I was looking at. Impatient, as the minutes ticked by, Mrs. Stern began tapping her pencil on the desk, creating more anxiety in me. Desperate for help, I began alternating glances from the photograph to Margaret. Pleading with my eyes, I was desperate for her to come forward and help me identify the set of pictures. However, Margaret completely avoided eye contract with me, unwilling to face Mrs. Stern with me.

"Quickly child, who is it? We don't have all day. The bell is about to ring and I need to pass out the rest of these pictures. Are these your pictures? Or not?" our teacher scolded as I stalled and squirmed.

Reluctantly, I finally mumbled, "I don't know."

Ms. Stern barked impatiently, "Speak up child! Speak up!"

"I don't know, Mrs. Stern," I said, embarrassed.

"What do you mean you don't know? Are you being impudent?" Mrs. Stern ridiculed in a snide voice. "Class, Katherine doesn't know if she is looking at herself or her sister."

The class roared with laughter, pointing at Margaret and me. My face turned crimson.

"You mean to tell me that you don't know if you are looking at yourself?" Mrs. Stern persisted.

With the entire class jeering and staring at me, Mrs. Stern announced as she held up the pictures once again, "Does anyone know who this is?"

Classmates began giving their opinion and before long every student was blurting out "Kat" or "Margaret" and changing their minds as quickly as they made their guesses known. Soon the class was in an uproar, jumping up and down blocking Margaret's view of the picture that our teacher was holding. Mrs. Stern had totally lost control of the situation, including the classroom discipline, normally her strong suit. With little patience left and trying desperately to get the class back to order, Mrs. Stern summoned Margaret to her desk to see if she could identify either set of pictures. Embarrassed for me and for herself, Margaret shuffled to the opposite side of Mrs. Stern's desk. Looking at the second set of pictures,

Margaret was as puzzled as I. What a frustrating dilemma this was becoming.

"Well, can you tell which set you are holding?" Mrs. Stern asked, directing her annoyance toward Margaret.

Margaret, without a sound, shook her head no.

Finally, I mustered up enough courage to ask, "May I look at the other pictures? Can Margaret and I swap pictures?"

As soon as the swap was made, we knew instantly the identity of each set.

We blurted out simultaneously, "This is you," and swapped the pictures again.

Flustered at the situation, Mrs. Stern grabbed both sets of pictures from our hands, studied them for differences, and seeing none, shook her head and asked, "Are you girls trying to make me look foolish? Is this just a joke y'all are playing? Well, it's not funny. Not funny at all. Here, take these and go sit down."

With Margaret in the lead, we hurried down the aisle with our backs to Mrs. Stern, grinning nervously at our classmates.

As Margaret sat down in my desk, I whispered to her back, "I was scared to death standin' up there by that mean ol' teacher. But it turned out OK, didn't it? Why did she have to embarrass us like that?"

When the last bell of the day rang, we rushed through the classroom door in a hurry to get away from Mrs. Stern. Our classmates patted us on the back and told us how much fun they had in class. They thanked us for the entertainment and openly hoped that we would do that again soon. We insisted that we were innocent of not knowing which picture was which. But despite what we said to them, they were convinced that we were playing a joke on Mrs. Stern.

"But it wasn't a joke," Margaret said, meaning it. "We were just as confused as y'all were."

Later as we were walking home, we relived the anxious moments of standing before Mrs. Stern. Eventually we laughed hysterically at what had taken place in class. Giggling, I said, "Can you believe she thought we were tryin' to trick her? I was really scared up there with her eyeballs starin' at me the whole time. She made me feel awful and real stupid. That mean ol' teacher."

"She doesn't like us and never has," Margaret chimed in. "It's 'cause we're twins. All she wanted to do was embarrass us. But she got what she deserved. The kids laughed at her, not at us."

I replied, "I really didn't know I was lookin' at my picture. Did you know you were lookin' at yours?"

"No. And she thought we were lyin'. It's funny how I knew your picture but I didn't know my own," Margaret said, now realizing how difficult it was for others to tell us apart.

Adding to her thought, I said, "I know. It's weird that I could tell who you were but I couldn't figure out I was lookin' at my picture the whole awful time. That's really weird!"

Later that night as I lay in bed, I thought about the events of the day. It seemed strange that I could identify Margaret's picture but not my own and vice versa. We understood, with clarity, why Mrs. Stern was having so much trouble telling us apart.

Months later on an early spring morning, two teams were being formed to play a game of kickball. Recess was my favorite time of the entire school day. Margaret and I stood together in the midst of the boys waiting to be chosen on one team or the other.

"Don't know why they don't let you be captain," Margaret whispered in my ear. "You're better than most all of 'em. Bet you're the first one picked on either team."

I dominated in sports with boys and girls alike. It made no difference which team Margaret was on, as I always took her place in the lineup. Being on the same team made it easier to switch on offense but playing on opposite teams posed a slightly more difficult problem. As the teams changed from offense to defense, we would meet each other in the infield, talk and switch places. I was always on offense when we were on separate teams and Margaret was always on defense – and did a pretty decent job.

On this particular spring morning we were chosen on different teams. Margaret was the pitcher for her team and was successful in catching the third out of the first inning. As the teams switched at the bottom half of the first inning, I ran toward Margaret to complete The Old Switcheroo.

Margaret caught me off guard and declared, "I'm gonna play the whole time with my team. I want to line up and kick the ball. You play with your team in the outfield today."

Surprised, I replied, "I can kick a home run for your team if you let me kick. Then everyone will think you are just as good as me. You watch. And the next time you come up to kick, all those ol' boys will be backin' up," I explained, trying desperately to convince her.

Reluctantly, Margaret gave in. As I stepped up to home base to kick for her, I loved the anticipation and rush of watching the ball sail over everyone's upheld arms. As I approached the plate, two outs, bases loaded, I knew this would be my finest hour. Margaret rolled a fastball toward the plate for me to kick, and kick it I did. It sailed over her head into center field. I rounded first base, second base, and third base, heading for home with lightning speed.

As Margaret caught the ball on relay, she ran toward home plate intent on tagging me out. She threw the ball at me as hard as she could and hit me square in the back of my knees. I fell hard before reaching home plate. I was the third out of the inning. Even though I had scored three runs, the humiliation of being taken out by Margaret was devastating. She proved to me that day that she could also play this game. I knew from that day forward that I would give her the opportunity to play whatever position she wanted. Actually, I was proud of her athletic abilities. And did she ever show me up!

We learned many tricks of the trade being identical twins that year – tricks that would benefit us for years to come. We learned that we could get away with many things, and used the experiences from the sixth grade as building blocks for future situations. Mainly, we learned that we could rely on each other and that being identical twins could definitely be useful in the future.

HAIRY LEGS

A milestone in every young girl's life is the ritual of shaving her legs for the very first time. Long-legged, hairy pre-teens at age eleven, we anticipated this momentous event. We were among the last to shave in our class, envying all of the other girls who had smooth, clean-shaven legs. We were by far the hairiest students – including the boys, some already approaching puberty.

We had pleaded with Mama for the past year to allow us to remove the unwanted hair from our legs. For the life of us, we couldn't see why she refused. Miracles do happen though. We were elated when she finally consented to our wishes on the second Saturday in March, a warm spring day in 1960, just two months before our sixth grade graduation. Not realizing the reasons for Mama's relenting, we were blindsided weeks later when we were forced to wear nylons and high heel shoes. Another first! Mama, in her wisdom, had sensed the impending disaster of pulling up nylons over our hairy legs.

Mama never explained her reasons to us. Mama was just that way. She just abruptly ended years of humiliation – or so we thought – one Saturday morning in late March.

Anticipating with an air of excitement the normalcy of looking like the other girls and fitting in somehow, we were jubilant at the notion of having hairless legs. But, puberty was just around the corner. Soon shaving legs would become just another ritual we would have to endure, an important step in the awkward transition from childhood through puberty into womanhood.

Awkward is kind, to say the least, but gangly and pimply is a better description – times two! Really, times three. Our brother, Bill, eleven months older, had a head start on puberty. His pubescent experiences served as advanced warning to our immediate future. However, being girls, there was still a lot more for us to learn and endure.

Marching down the long hallway to the girls' bathroom, we followed one step behind Mama, anxious to begin the process. Kat and I entertained our own ideas of the outcome, only glancing now and then at one another, wondering at the other's thoughts. Nothing was secret in our house. As we prepared to shave our hairy legs for the first time, word spread quickly throughout our household of seven. We had an entourage of curious siblings.

Breaking the curtain of silence between us, Kat whispered in my ear, "I'm goin' first this time. I always let you go first."

Agitated, I fired back, "What? You don't let me. You always make me go first."

"I do not!" Kat said with an air of irritation louder than intended.

The short spat caught Mama's attention, but before she could reprimand us our five-year old brother, Allan, chimed in questioning, "Shavin'? Are y'all shavin' your faces like Daddy? Can I watch? I never saw hair on your faces. I didn't know girls shaved!"

Kirk and Bill were grouped around Allan. Bill responded to Allan's question, "No, you silly boy, girls don't shave their faces, they shave their legs."

Allan's eyes drifted from our faces to our legs and squatting to get a closer look, he reached out and pulled the coarse hair on Kat's leg, saying, "You're gonna get all that hair off? Wow! I wanna watch. Can I?"

Kat slapped his hand and shoved him backward. With angry eyes flashing, she dismissed the gawkers with a no nonsense command, "Get lost, 'cause you're not gonna watch."

Shutting the door in the face of our curious siblings, we turned to Mama for our first instruction. Mama filled the tub with warm water and gathered the tools needed for the task at hand.

While she assembled the razor, extra blades, soap and towels, Mama ordered, "One of you get undressed and get in the tub."

"I'm goin' first." Kat answered quickly and began fumbling with the buttons on her blouse and wiggling out of her shorts.

She knew about shaving since she had been shaving under her arms for nearly a year. In her mind this made her an expert in razor management.

"You don't have to show me how to do this, Mama. I already know how to do it. Just watch me," Kat said haughtily.

Staring momentarily at Kat, Mama, then, without comment, returned to her step-by-step instructions. "Now pay attention, Katherine. You don't know as much as you think you do," she added facing Kat. "Are you listening?"

Unwilling to meet Mama's stare, Kat nodded and muttered meekly, "Yes, Ma'am."

"Now get in the tub and take the soap and lather one of your hairy legs. You are to shave no further than one inch above your knees. Demonstrating an inch with her thumb and forefinger, she added, pinning both of us with her eyes, "Do both of understand me?"

We answered in unison Mama's directive with enthusiastic nods. I sat on the toilet waiting for the events to unfold. With a heightened sense of curiosity, I watched as Mama sat on the side of the tub waiting while Kat lathered up.

Impatient to have the task complete, Mama rose and as she left warned, "Make sure you take short strokes. That razor blade is very sharp."

With Mama out of the bathroom, we relished the thought of finishing this very personal mission together without Mama hanging over our heads.

It seemed surreal as I watched Kat sitting in a bathtub half filled with clean water. We were two excited eleven-year old girls ready to remove the unsightly hair from our legs.

Eager to start, Kat ordered, "Get the razor ready for me. Make sure it's not comin' loose at the bottom. Twist it so it's real tight then put it on the side of the tub, right here while I finish gettin' this soap all over my leg. It's takin' a long time to do this."

Diagnosing the problem I suggested, "Your leg got too dry. Wet it again so the soap will go on better."

Splashing water onto her leg, Kat worked up a good lather. Once she was satisfied with the right consistency of soap to hair, Kat dropped the soap into the water, and, as it floated off, she reached for the razor.

With her back against the rear of the tub and a long leg stretched before her, Kat picked up the razor, hesitated, grinned at me and took the first long swipe from her ankle to knee. With an air of excitement, she began scraping the long, black, thick, straight hair from her leg. I was observing from the throne, recalling all of Mama's instructions as I watched the hair miraculously disappear from Kat's leg. After a few long, quick swipes of the razor, she was bleeding and the blade was clogged.

"Give me another blade. This one is stuffed with hair stickin' out everywhere. I can't use it anymore. See? Look," she demanded as she shoved the razor up under my nose.

"Loosen it up at the bottom like Mama said and swish it around in the water. That'll clear out all that hair," I instructed.

"I didn't know Mama said that. Good thing you were listenin'," Kat said.

I couldn't tell if she was really appreciative or being bossy.

With a quick comeback I responded, "You never listen. She also said to take short strokes."

Kat glared at me with a surprised look saying, "She did? Guess that's why I'm bleedin'. And it stings real bad, too."

Startled at the beads of blood on her leg, Kat decided to slow down the process by attempting to follow Mama's instructions. This method didn't work either. The blade was too sharp and the hair was too dense to make a difference. Two razor blades later, she had one smooth leg and was sitting in a tub of bloody water with mounds of hair clinging to her and the inside of the tub. Ready to begin the second leg, Kat noticed that the bar of soap had disappeared. Unable to see it in the hair-laden, blood-stained water, she searched for it with her hands. She squealed and lurched forward as suddenly from behind her back, a 'fuzzy thing' floated into her peripheral vision.

Squirming quickly away, Kat splashed the 'thing' to the back of the tub and yelled, "Kill it, Margaret. It's a spider. Kill it! Get it before it gets me! Hurry!"

At that moment Allan yelled from outside the door in his little boy voice, "Mama, come fast! There's a spider in the tub with Kat."

Before I could open the door to silence him, Mama stepped in to the bathroom to investigate.

Staring in disbelief at the scene before her, she muttered, "Good grief, would you look at that?" She shook her head, turned and left.

When Mama opened the door, Allan popped his head in exclaiming excitedly, "Let me see. I wanna see."

I jumped off the toilet, pushed him backward, and slammed the door shut, admonishing, "Get out of here and leave us alone. Get!"

Kat yelled, "Go away or you'll be sorry."

I returned my attention to Kat who had snatched a bath rag from the floor to use as a shield when Allan entered. At the same time she was attempting to keep the floating blob at bay.

Trying to contain my laughter as I watched from the throne, I blurted out, "That 'thing' is the soap. It's just covered with your hair."

Getting down to eye level with the 'thing' Kat couldn't believe what she was seeing. The white of the soap could barely be detected through the thick layers of hair stuck to it.

Kat grinned sheepishly and floated the so-called spider to the back of the tub and demanded, "You need to pick it up and clean it off so I can use it on my other leg."

I wouldn't go near it, replying, "Are you kiddin' me? No way! I'm not touchin' that ol' thing. You pick it up yourself. It's your hair."

Very carefully Kat picked up the hairy wad between her thumb and index finger and swished it in the murky water. Nothing happened. Turning on the faucet to rinse it, she finally began picking the hair off one by one until enough of the soap shown through. Then she began lathering the remaining leg. Shaving the second leg didn't go any better than the first. Blood seemed to seep from all pores and hair continued to fill the filthy bath water. Two legs down, two to go.

Bloody water drained SLOWLY from the bathtub, leaving us amazed to find most of Kat's long, black hairs still clinging to the tub's surface – and to her! Squatting under the running faucet, Kat managed to remove most of the clinging hair from her body. She finally rose to get out of the tub, eager to dry off so she could feel her soft legs. Even though her legs were blood splotched, Kat kept rubbing them, unable to believe what she was feeling. With wide eyes, I was amazed at the contrast between Kat's legs and mine – slick versus coarse and hairy! We stared at before and after.

Knowing I was next, I was now excited about getting started and blurted out, "I'm glad you went first. Now I know how to do it the right way."

When there was no response from Kat, I looked to see why. In her euphoric state, she was moving her hands up and down over her smooth legs singing off key, "You ain't nothin' butta hound dog, just a cryin' all the time."

I interrupted her utopian world, demanding, "You gotta clean the tub so I can shave."

Ignoring my request, she asked excited, "Wanna feel my legs? They feel so smooth. Feel 'em."

Looking at her bloody legs I blurted, "No! Not now. You gotta clean the tub so I can shave."

"Well, you gotta help me," Kat insisted, dressing quickly as we stared at the tub and then at each other. "How we gonna do it?"

We looked around the small bathroom for cleaning supplies. There was nothing to use to get do the job done. Obviously Mama hadn't anticipated the disastrous results since she left no scouring pads, or Comet, or instructions on how to clean the plethora of hair clinging to the sides of the tub.

"Here, use this," Kat suggested as she pulled a streamer of toilet paper off the roll. "Wipe the sides of it off with this, then toss it in the toilet. Don't flush it 'till we are through."

"Why?" I asked curiously.

"'Cause we don't want Mama hearin' the toilet flush a lot. She'll come back in and see what we're doin'."

"OK," I replied, fully understanding Kat's reasoning.

"And look, there's not much toilet paper left, so get all you can every time you wipe."

"What are you gonna do while I'm cleanin' up your mess?" I asked a bit ticked off.

"You see that bar of soap? I'm gonna pick off all that hair stuck to it," Kat said curtly.

"OK. OK. OK. You do that. I'll clean the tub," I quickly agreed.

On my knees, bending over the tub, I began the tedious chore. It was no easy task, but it had to be done before I could begin drawing my water. Swiping at the soap-scummed hair, I looked up to see Kat leap onto the toilet lid to open Mama's make-up drawer.

"What are you doin' now?" I asked, irritated.

"I'm gonna grab Mama's tweezers so I can pick all this hair off this soap," she answered. Hand the soap to me."

Miffed, I twisted around, tore off a few sheets of toilet paper, scooped up the nasty soap and deposited it in Kat's open palm, with my own directive, "OK. But hurry up. See if there's more toilet paper up there. I'm almost out. You gotta get down off that so I can throw this stuff in the toilet."

Kat jumped to the floor, tweezers in hand, and opened the lid. I tossed the first of many wads of hair-covered toilet paper into the bowl. For the next fifteen minutes Kat tweezed at the lavatory and I wiped down the tub until there was no more toilet paper left. Resting on the side of the tub, I threw the last bit of toilet paper into the bowl and gasped at the mound of tissue and hair floating there.

"Look," I said, interrupting Kat's hair-plucking job. "Look at all this stuff in the toilet. Do you think it will all go down at one time? What do we do if it overflows? We'll be in big trouble and you know it."

"Naw, it'll flush. Watch this," Kat said confidently as she pushed the lever down. "See, it's gone."

On close inspection I replied, "Not all of it. There's still lots of hair floating around in there. Here, I'll flush it again."

Grabbing my arm, Kat said, "No. Not now. We'll do that later. Are you through cleanin' the tub?"

"No. Ran out of toilet paper," I said knowing why she didn't want the toilet flushed again.

Kat reached across to the towel rack and tossed me a bath rag saying, "Clean the rest with this. Rinse it out under the faucet when it gets full of hair. I'm 'bout through with this soap. Then I'll help you."

Obeying Kat's orders, I returned to cleaning the remainder of the tub. And before long I had the tub clean enough to begin filling it with water. Several minutes later, Kat gave the soap a final rinse and tossed it into the tub where I was now sitting.

"Here you go, lather up," Kat said cheerfully as the soap splashed into the water.

I grabbed the soap and began rubbing it on my legs, trying to work up a good foamy lather.

Kat coached from the sideline, sitting high and mighty on the toilet seat giving her expert advice, "Instead of soapin' your legs, try gettin' lots of soap on your hands and then rub your hands on your legs."

Ignoring her directives, I continued rubbing the soap across, up and down my leg, making no progress. Finally I picked up the Ivory soap and after working up a thick lather, applied it to my leg.

"See. I told you that would work better. Not any hair on your hands. So it's easier to get a lather. Can't get a good lather on those hairy legs. You should listen to me. I know what I'm talkin' about. Remember, I just did mine and they still sting but they feel so good. Can't wait for you to finish yours," Kat gloated as she rubbed some of Mama's Jergens lotion on her smooth but still bleeding legs.

Perturbed at Kat's snide remarks, I took a deep breath and picked up the razor, but it was still clogged with Kat's hair.

"Here," I said irritably. "Clean this out at the sink. It's stuffed with your hair."

Kat grabbed the razor and unscrewing it at the bottom, dumped the gross blade in the trash can.

After rinsing the razor, she inserted a new blade, screwed it in place and handed it to me saying, "Remember, this is a new blade. And it's sharp. Be careful and make short strokes. You don't wanna be bleedin' like me."

Minding Mama's instructions, as I always did, I took short measured strokes, inch by inch up my right leg to the stopping point above the knee. We looked at the result and laughed at the site – a reverse Mohawk!

But quickly laughter turned to shock as the blood began to seep from all pores where the razor nicked the skin.

I winced at the sight and with tears welling up in my eyes, whined, "I just cut open all my goose bumps, and it burns!"

Unsympathetic to my pain, Kat urged, "Stop bein' a sissy. You just got started. Now finish it. When you get through it's great. Keep goin'. I'll rinse the razor for you, so your leg doesn't have to touch the water."

I braved the pain with Kat's insistence. She ignored the tears and pressed me to finish the job. Once finished, the dread of lowering my cut up legs into the water hung over me. I stalled as long as I could before Kat snatched her bloody towel from the floor, reached over the tub, covered my legs and then unsympathetically shoved them into the water.

I screamed as tears streamed down my face, "Ouch! Stop! That feels like a thousand bees stingin' my legs."

"I know. But you gotta finish. It'll feel better in a minute," Kat lied.

I jumped out of the water and toweled off, hoping the bleeding and stinging would stop if my legs were dry.

Trying to stop my crying, Kat urged, "Here. Put this lotion on. It'll help."

As I applied the lotion, more pain shot through my legs. I scowled at Kat but continued applying the lotion as it really did seem to help cool off my burning legs. Finally, we gaped in awe at our hairless lower limbs. How wonderful it was to be clean shaven!

I asked, "Do you think we hafta to do this every day for the rest of our lives?"

Kat responded, "We'll hafta to wait 'til tomorrow to see how fast it grows back. Look at the tub. We've gotta get it clean so we can go out and play. Come on. Let's get this mess cleaned up so we can get outta here."

Allan knocked on the door and, hoping for permission to enter, asked, "Can I come in now?"

Opening the door and gesturing him to enter, Kat said, "Sure. Come on in."

Allan took in the scene and gasped, "What happened to your legs? They're bloody and look at those towels and what happened to the tub? Did it hurt? Let me feel."

Kat swatted Allan's hand away as he reached out to touch her leg.

She picked him up, slung him onto her right hip and said in her most manipulative, sweet voice, "I'll let you touch my legs if you help us clean up the tub. It's not really that hard. All you have to do is get inside the tub and wipe it down with this rag. Margaret will show you how to do it."

"Really?" Allan questioned.

"Really," Kat answered in a sugary tone as she kissed Allan on the cheek.

We cleaned the bathroom spick and span and to Mama's liking. Then Allan, Kat and I gathered at the picnic table on the back patio where Kirk and Bill were playing "Go Fish". Kat and I sat down on top of the table dangling smooth-shaven legs over the end.

Bill glanced at our legs which now had hundreds of beaded blood stains all over them. Then realizing something was different, looked more closely. He started to say something, but closed his mouth, looked into our faces and asked with feigned innocence, "What happened to y'all? You look like a chicken with all its feathers plucked off. "

He stood and pranced around the patio making clucking sounds and flapping his wings. Angry at Bill teasing her, Kat jumped from the table and ran for him. With just barely a head start, Bill took off down the hill toward the creek at the back of the property with Kat hot on his tail. Pretty soon both were out of sight.

Within minutes Kat returned, out of breath, and reported, "He's crossed the creek and won't be back for a while."

As she came closer and closer to me, I was horrified to see that her legs did look freaky. That's the moment I realized mine did also. I looked down at my knees. On closer examination I was shocked at the contrast that existed at the dividing line – that line right above the knee where the shave ended and the hair began. It was as though we had cut bangs straight across the top of our knees.

Kat immediately recognized we had a real problem – a real self-image crisis. She motioned me to follow her. Looking back to see that we were not being followed, Kat sniffled, almost crying, "This is awful isn't it? What are we gonna do 'bout it?"

"Yeah, I thought this would be the best day of our lives. But it's not. We're worse off than before, you know? What can we do 'bout it? Everyone is gonna make fun of us. We'll be wearin' shorts all summer long and get teased by everyone."

"This is real embarrasin'. Real embarrasin' for sure," Kat mumbled as tears trickled down her cheek. "And we have to wear swimsuits. How are we gonna go swimmin' lookin' like this?" The true impact hit. We would be the laughing stocks at the pool, our pre-teen minds knew. We could already hear the howls.

We were silent for a long time, walking hand in hand toward our secret hiding place among the trees in the woods. We knew we had to solve the problem, but how?

We worried with our dilemma as spring turned to summer and school was out. Our present predicament was obvious to even the youngest, wearing shorts brought laughter from our brothers and sister, adding to our misery. There was no doubt in our minds that we looked weird. We could look at each other and know just how embarrassed we should be. The first problem we faced was getting into the country club swimming pool the first day of summer vacation without anyone noticing our legs. After many hours of deliberation, we came up with two plausible solutions: The Shorts Theory and The Towel Theory. With the Shorts Theory – meaning our shorts were on over our swimsuits – we planned to remove our shorts as quickly as possible and jump immediately into the pool. Having practiced and timed this routine at home, we discarded this theory. In the rush to get the shorts off, our big feet tripped us up. We couldn't depend on a smooth delivery, so we abandoned it. Besides, the shorts weren't long enough to cover up the problem.

The Towel Theory, on the other hand, worked out well during practice sessions in the privacy of our room, but we feared that it might not work at the crowded swimming pool with all those people around.

"Do you think this is gonna work when we get to the pool?" I asked, skeptical.

"Yeah, we can pull it off real easy. Don't worry 'bout it. We've practiced a lot and it worked real good," Kat said confidently.

Having driven all five of us to the pool the first day it opened, Mama warned, "I expect all of you to behave and don't break any of the rules. Do you understand, Katherine?"

Avoiding looking directly at Mama, Kat replied meekly, "Yes, Ma'am."

"Margaret, are you feeling okay?" Mama glared at me. "You look as if you don't feel well."

"Oh, yes, Ma'am," I assured her, "we feel okay, don't we, Kat?"

"Huh? Oh sure, we're okay. Let's go swimmin', Margaret. Whatcha waitin' for?" Kat said with feigned bravado.

Before Mama could respond, we jumped out of the car and ran for the back of the line that had formed at the entrance gate to the pool.

"What was that all 'bout?" Kat tightened the towel draped around her waist.

"You know that peanut butter sandwich we ate for lunch?" I whispered. "Well, I thought it was 'bout to come back up on the ride over here. I'm real nervous 'bout all this and my stomach is upset."

"Oh, you don't have to worry. It's gonna be real easy to do. Just follow what I do and you'll be fine."

We stayed at the back of the line so as not to draw attention to ourselves. We held our towels tight around our waists. All our girlfriends ahead of us in line were showing off their new swimsuits, but we avoided modeling ours.

The lifeguard blew his whistle which announced that the pool was about to open, and as he unlocked the gate, declared, "No running or you will sit out for fifteen minutes. Make sure you read all the rules posted on the board."

The crowd moved quickly through the gate and jumped into the pool, filling the air with screams of delight and loud laughter. By the time Kat and I got through the gate, Kirk, Allan, and Bill were already splashing water in each other's face. We decided to sit at the wading pool to figure out our strategy.

"Look at everyone havin' fun. I'm ready to jump in, aren't you?" I asked expectantly.

"Shallow end or deep end?" Kat asked.

"Right here at the shallow end," I responded.

"On the count of three, throw off your towel as quick as you can. You know, like we practiced at home. And walk as fast as you can and jump in. We'll go at the same time. I'll count to three. Ready?" Kat asked. "Okay, one, two, three go!"

We flung off our towels. By the time they hit the fence we were hitting the water.

The three feet of water in the shallow end covered us to the waist. We were comfortable knowing that our strange-looking legs were hidden from view. So we played there with Allan and Kirk the entire afternoon.

With time getting closer to five o'clock, Kat and I began to focus on how we were going to retrieve our towels without others noticing us. We had not even considered how we could get out of the pool without drawing attention. We had focused solely on getting into the pool, not out.

At four forty-five the lifeguard blew his whistle, signaling the time for all swimmers to get out. Kat and I procrastinated while others around us were exiting the pool. Finally, we were the only two left, but still we had no solution.

With a stroke of genius, Kat summoned Allan saying, "Bring Margaret her towel."

While Allan obeyed the order, Kat gave me some specific instructions, "After Allan gives you your towel, get out and bring me mine. Hold the towel open wide so when I get to the top of the ladder you can wrap it around me."

As the weeks went by, we became more comfortable with our surroundings and used our towels as shields whenever we entered and exited the pool. Thanks to Allan, our unknown conspirator.

That was the only summer of our lives that we were grateful for school to begin. It couldn't start fast enough. For, you see, we wore only dresses in 1959 and we could hide our half-hairy, half-smooth legs.

"By the time we have to wear shorts and swimsuits next year we have to get rid of the rest of this hair," Kat said with conviction. "We can start shavin' a little higher and higher each time so by next year we have no hair all the way up to our…what's it called?"

HIGH HEEL BOOT CAMP

Henry Higgins of *My Fair Lady* would have had his greatest chAllange coaching the King Twins in the art of walking "properly." Our Mama's strong determination to make us into ladies included, among other things, how to walk in high heels. We spent countless boring hours of intense training enduring Mama's scheduled daily practices. The sessions began in early spring before our sixth grade graduation in May. In teaching us to walk like ladies, Mama hoped to save us from embarrassing moments as we made our way down the aisle, up the steps, and across the stage to receive our diplomas. To keep two graceless daughters from tripping and stumbling while debuting in high heels, Mama programmed detailed lessons taking hours of practice each day. While many of our friends took piano lessons, dance lessons, or baton lessons from accomplished tutors, we took walking lessons from an equally accomplished instructor – Mama. By the time we reached the sixth grade we felt fortunate to have escaped all types of lessons, but in fact, they had really just begun.

High Heel Boot Camp began in March 1960 and continued for several weeks, consuming all of our after-school playtime. Instead of our usual activities in the yard, Mama not only required but expected us to practice walking while chanting as we practiced, "Shoulders up, stomach in, chin out, head high, feet straight." And, at the same time, she expected us to master GLIDING!

That asked a lot of two pigeon-toed, eleven-year old tomboys! We had our own reasons for slumping and watching our feet. First of all, we were tall and gangly, towering over our classmates. Standing up straight and holding our shoulders up made us feel like bean poles, so we slumped, wanting to better fit in with our peers.

Secondly, we never looked straight ahead when we walked; instead our attention centered on our over-sized, pigeon-toed feet as we kicked stones and bodocks down the sidewalks and driveway every day. As one can imagine, our Buster Brown saddle oxfords took the brunt of the punishment. Having spent years walking pigeon-toed in those sturdy shoes, walking feet-straight would prove to be an almost impossible task to accomplish in just two months.

The third complication we faced that spring as we began gliding lessons focused on walking straight instead of pigeon-toed. I walked with a slight impediment, but Kat walked with a severe one. How Kat could put one pigeon-toed foot in front of the other and not stumble over her size 9 shoe amazed me. Mama had two obstacles to overcome: us, two girls with absolutely no natural ability or inclination to walk ladylike. After years of wearing saddle oxfords, we knew no other way than how we had always walked. Walking in clunky saddle oxfords was one thing, but Mama had even bigger plans – gliding faultlessly across the stage at graduation.

GLIDING was a complicated process. We had to learn how to walk properly because a return trip to Neilson's in two months' time would find us proud owners of a pair of white patent leather high heels. Nonetheless, training did begin on a regular routine that spring before graduation. We were not accustomed to acting like ladies and certainly not walking like ladies. I didn't fare so badly since I seemed to learn the process more easily than Kat. She, on the other hand, was barely trainable. Between the two of us, Mama had her work cut out all right, as neither of us were willing participants. We were Eliza Doolittle, times two!

Picture this, the first afternoon of High Heel Boot Camp. We arrived home after school in seven-month old, comfortable saddle oxfords to practice walking in fancy high heels.

But before we could begin, there were other tasks to consider. Immediately we found piled high on the toilet seat in our bathroom these assorted items: an encyclopedia, a girdle, a garter belt, a pair of our Mama's discarded black patent leather one-inch heels, a pair of nylons with only a few runs in them, a shoehorn, and a razor. Kat lifted her dress to straddle the side of the tub and scanned the items with disgust. She held up each article for inspection. Everything seemed to have a use except the razor, which Kat placed on the back of the toilet.

Taking control she snapped up the second item on the stack, tossing it my way. As the shoehorn clattered to the tile floor, Kat shook her head, disappointed that I hadn't caught it. I sat on the cool floor to retrieve the shoehorn, angry at the situation in which we found ourselves. Kat picked the girdle up, grimaced and then tossed it my way. Next, she held the stockings at arm's length looped over the end of each forefinger and flipped them over her left shoulder into the tub.

She mused, as the second one floated into the tub, "Huh, wonder how you get these things on?"

Giggles outside the bathroom door alerted us that someone was spying on us. Kat slammed the door hard, cutting off all communication between us and the rest of the household.

Turning her attention back to the diminishing stack on the toilet seat, she pitched the patent leather heels over her head, each landing in the tub behind her with a resounding thud. The next order of business was the garter belt. Bringing it to eye level, she examined it, not knowing front from back, which way was right side up, inside out or upside down. Confusion on her face revealed she had no idea what the garter belt was, how to put it on, or even what part of her body it would cover.

I studied her puzzled face, stifling a laugh as she tossed it toward me. It barely missed my lap and landed squarely on my head, its straps and hooks dangling against my face. Scowling, I jerked it off my head for a closer look, equally puzzled at the contraption and the actual mechanics of putting it on. Seeing no use for it, I tossed it aside.

Weary of wasting time, Kat picked up Volume A and reached over the toilet and laid it on the bathroom scales, astonished at its weight. We knew right off what its function was because Mama put books on our heads from time to time hoping we'd learn how to walk poised. Mouths agape, we realized that heavy book was meant to be balanced on our heads.

Contemplating the absurdity of the situation, Kat groused, "I hate this." More forcefully, she then demanded, "Pick up that ol' book and put it somewhere."

Not wanting to anger her any more than she already was, I dragged Volume A onto the bathroom floor, scooting it to my side where several of the items had already been carelessly discarded. We stared morosely at the floor, wondering why in the world we were in this dilemma. Preying on our minds was the stark realization that we had to swap our now comfortable saddle oxfords for a pair of Mama's worn-out high heel shoes. Retrieving the tub-tossed heels, I gave one to Kat, keeping the other one for closer examination. Kat did a little comparison herself by placing the pointed toe of the high heel against her shoe-clad foot.

Thoughtfully, Kat stared at me, grumbling, "This'll never work. Not in a million years. Where are my toes gonna go? No way can I cram 'em in these ol' things."

Before we tried on the shoes, we had to figure out how to wear a garter belt correctly and to maneuver the nylons into the garter belt hooks – not an easy task for two novices. The previous evening, we had been given detailed instructions, for Mama spent what seemed an eternity giving step-by-step lessons on exactly how to wear each piece of intimate apparel. To our regret, we paid little attention to her at the time. Now, as I stretched the garter belt like an accordion, we wished we had been more attentive as we struggled to remember the sequence. Kat insisted the garter belt went on over her head since it had an opening like Bill's t-shirt, but I argued that it was feet first like our shorts. So we took renewed interest in the garter belt with its four hooks attached to four straps hanging from the garment.

We heard laughter from outside the bathroom window and knew Bill and Allan were spying on us again. Quickly glancing out the window, we found ourselves staring directly into Allan's eyes as he rocked back and forth on Bill's shoulders. Knowing they were caught red handed, Bill, staggering under the weight of Allan, fled as fast as his crane-like legs would move. With the extra forty-five pounds on his shoulders, Bill reeled backward, tumbling his passenger to the ground. In a bid to escape, Bill fell hard, sprawling on top of the smaller Allan.

At the exact same time, Kat raised the screen-less bathroom window. She snatched the garter belt from my hands, grasped the elasticized straps in her right hand, stretched the body of the garter belt with her left hand slingshot style, faced the open window and shot it across the side yard to within inches of Bill's face. Astonished at the distance the garment traveled, Kat hesitated momentarily, and then scurried out the window in a race with the boys to retrieve it. Snatching the improvised slingshot from Bill, Kat tossed it through the window as she struggled to reenter the bathroom the same way she exited. Bill had a hold on Kat's legs so I leaned over the window sill, grabbed Kat's arms and hoisted her through the opening, landing on my back in the bathtub with Kat sprawled on top of me.

Laughing at our antics, we scrambled to stand, straightened our dresses, and straddled the side of the tub facing each other. Kat turned on the cold water in the tub, took a long swig, wetting the nylons and shoes. She turned to face me, wiping water from her face with the back of her hand, then picked up the garter belt, and grinned. We both stared at the garter belt, seeing it with renewed respect.

Kat flexed it, imagining its future use, and finally commented dryly, "I'm gonna use this as my secret weapon. It'll make a great sling shot."

Refocusing on the task at hand, Kat retrieved the wet stockings from the tub, held them and the garter belt up between us, and studied them with intensity as if seeing them for the first time.

Kat waved the belt and nylons at me and ordered, "Put 'em on. I'm not gonna put 'em on 'til I have to. You go first." She dropped them on the floor and asked, "How did Mama say you put 'em on?"

I couldn't respond because I couldn't remember a thing from Mama's instructions. Delaying the torture as long as possible, I looked away from Kat to study the scattered clothing on the floor. We realized there was nothing to be gained by further delay. Perched on the side of the tub, we began the ordeal by removing shoes and socks, permeating the small space with stale odors of sweaty feet and dirty socks. Fanning our hands back and forth and gasping for fresh air, we dashed for the open window in an effort to breathe the March breeze. Tiring of time wasted, Kat yanked me back in, shoved the pile of clothing into my arms and pushed me onto the toilet seat. Unable to delay the inevitable any longer, I slipped one of the wet nylons onto my foot.

"So far, so good. This is easy," I said, giving little thought to what I was doing.

As I pulled the stocking up my right leg, it met with considerable resistance. It had been almost twenty-four hours since I had last shaved. The thick hair stubbles on my leg immediately caused additional runs in the stocking and kept it from rolling smoothly up to meet the garter hooks. Even worse, I had forgotten to put on the garter belt. Time to rethink and start over.

Watching me struggle and learning from my efforts, Kat reached over my right shoulder and grabbed the razor from the back of the toilet. Waving it in the air between us, she and I realized, at that moment, that step one must be the shaving our legs. This revelation shocked us back to the reality of having to take a bath in order to shave. Rebelling at the thought of having to take a bath at this time of day, Kat concocted a wild plan.

She handed over the razor to me with a wicked gleam in her eyes and ordered, "Dry shave."

I had never done this before. I considered the request momentarily then replied, "Okay, why not?"

I readily agreed with Kat that taking a bath in order to shave seemed unnecessary. Hanging one leg at a time over the edge of the tub, I scraped the stubble as quickly as possible. Thinking ahead to the next step, I paid little attention to what was happening as I hurried through this stage of the training. Then I realized too late that Mama had inserted a new blade into the razor. We exchanged astonished looks at the end result – blood-splotched legs.

"Oh well, what's done is done," Kat sneered as she shrugged off the mishap, splashed water onto my bloody legs and tossed me a towel.

Teary eyed at the stinging pain, I wiped my legs dry as Kat threw the girdle, garter belt, stockings and heels at me.

"Put 'em on," she ordered out of frustration.

Dejected, I lifted my skirt, shimmied into the girdle, feeling my blood supply cut off at the waist. Breathless, I put the garter belt on and began the struggle with the stockings. I was standing on one foot while trying to get the other foot into the stocking. I lost my balance, and fell into Kat who was sitting on the side of the tub. Again we found ourselves toppled into the tub, laughing hysterically. Exasperated, I regained my composure, plopped on the side of the tub and slowly guided a nylon up my left leg. I snapped the front hook, stood up, turned my back to Kat and waited for her to hook the one in the back.

Not wanting to touch my bloody legs, she fumbled with the back hook and in frustration finally gave up. This ritual was repeated with the right leg. Unknowingly, I was about to GLIDE with half-hooked nylons. Resuming my place on the tub, I tried stuffing my feet into high heel shoes that were at least a size too small. I traded places with Kat and sat on the toilet using the side of the tub for leverage. With the aid of a shoehorn I forced my foot into the shoe, cringing in agony as my five toes mutated into one at the point of the shoe. Standing seemed impossible as I struggled to balance in the one-inch heels. I stumbled into the hallway where an audience of three was perched in the threshold of our bedroom door waiting for the show to begin. The familiar twenty-foot hallway now seemed as long as an airport runway as I began the long trip to the other end.

From behind, Kat placed the encyclopedia on my head. Before attempting to take one tentative step at a time I had to grab the heavy book with both hands to keep it steady. Slowly I lowered my hands, lest it fall. Standing soldier-like, arms pasted at my sides, I advanced down the hall, one shaky step at a time.

Kat offered her support by sarcastically reciting, "Shoulders up, stomach in, chin out, head high, feet straight and GLIDE," as she sat with Kirk, Allan, and Bill to watch the show.

Copying Kat's antics, the others chimed in chanting, pointing, gawking and cheering me on as I made feeble attempts at GLIDING. Kat teased and chanted behind my back, thinking how easy it looked, not realizing how impossible it would be when it was her turn. To accomplish one of the assigned tasks would truly have been amazing, but to do all of them at the same time seemed impossible. Gliding didn't come easy with oversized feet stuffed into high heel shoes, toes pinched to the point that my feet bowed. On my return trip as I was approaching the finish line, Bill stuck out his bony foot, tripping me. The stockings popped loose, the encyclopedia went flying, and the high heels caved in as I fell hard into Kat, landing solidly prone on the floor. A chorus of laughter erupted from the onlookers.

But despite the fall, the high-heel shoes never budged from my feet. The stockings dangling from my knee caps were glued in place with dried blood.

Even though I was stunned, these thoughts kept reeling in my mind, *How am I gonna get these nylons off my legs? Will my toes ever quit aching? And will I ever be rid of this ol' girdle and breathe again?*

Seeing the top of the stockings curled around my ankles and the remainder of them stuck to my legs, Kat turned away laughing, "I didn't hook 'em because they had your cooties on 'em. I wasn't gonna touch those nasty things."

No problem, I thought as I slowly pried the shoes from my feet, and threw them at the grinning Kat.

"It's your turn, anyway," I snapped.

Allan crawled within inches of my aching feet, astonished to see the red-splotched hosiery and my toes apparently fused together as one unit. Seeing that I was in agony, he quickly reached out and ripped the now dry, blood-stained stocking down my left leg, bringing a scream of pain from my lips and tears to my eyes.

Startled, Allan fell back, muttering, "Sorry. I'm sorry. What did I do? Did I hurt you? Sorry, sorry."

Kat was quick to placate him, responding to his questions, "Don't worry, Allan. She's not hurt. She's just bein' a sissy."

Glaring at Kat, I blurted out, "You just wait 'til it's your turn. Then we'll see who's a sissy."

I shook my left leg in the air and blew on the fresh wounds for relief while pondering how to get the nylon off my right leg. Kat suggested that I go to the tub and wet my leg down and then the nylon would slip off easily.

Before I could get to the bathtub, I had to figure out how to stand and quickly turned my attention to the dull throb, surprised to see all ten toes wiggling. Feeling sorry for me, Allan sidled back to massage my aching feet. Tingling toes reassured me that the feeling was indeed returning as I stood somewhat tentatively, fearful of falling. Hobbling gingerly as the aching abated, I abandoned the idea of going to the tub in order to concentrate on getting out of the girdle. I unceremoniously wiggled out of the garter belt before tackling the bigger problem. I then began tugging at the stiff garment, pulling it back and forth, exerting all effort to get out of its clutches.

I begged for mercy, exclaiming, "Get me outta this thing. It's gotta hold of me. Someone help me. I'm suffocatin'."

Intently watching my struggles and acting on my cries for help, Allan reached out and haltingly, tugged at the girdle, trying to help. When that plan failed he yanked harder, clasping his hands on the girdle at both sides of my waist.

He hung on for dear life and shouted, "Look, I'm swingin'."

Everyone turned to see Allan's legs bent at the knees swinging between my legs as though he was holding onto a swing set bar about to skin the cat.

I screamed, "Stop, stop. Get off me. You're killin' me. Get away from me."

We toppled to the floor and wide-eyed Allan scooted out of the way. Worried that the garment was permanently affixed to my body, I enlisted everyone's help to peel it off. Soon all hands were tugging at the rigid girdle as I squirmed and twisted with renewed effort. As I lay on the floor, gasping for air, I felt like a trapped animal wanting to be free of this contraption. Eventually the joint effort was successful as the garment was slowly peeled away, bringing with it the second nylon. In agony, I cried out as blood oozed from the fresh wounds. Allan waved all the garments over his head as prized trophies and then tossed them into the tub. Following behind him, I turned on the cold water to wash my bloody legs off, while everyone else collapsed onto the hall floor, clutching their stomachs in pained laughter.

After a bit, Kat regained her composure and having learned from my mistakes, decided to take a different approach. Looking closely at the girdle, she stated emphatically, "I'm not gonna wear that ol' thing. It almost killed you. Anyway, it's too wet to wear. I'm just gonna wear that thing with those dangly things hangin' off it."

"Mama said you have to wear 'em both, so you have to put both of 'em on," I admonished, returning to the hallway to confront her.

Kat rebutted. "I bet Mama said use one or the other, not both. Look here, both of the garments have these dangly things that hold up the nylons. You must not have listened to Mama when she told you how to use 'em."

Snatching the remaining garments as she retreated to the bathroom, Kat grabbed me by the arm en route. As I hobbled in tow behind her, she slammed and locked the bathroom door, precluding onlookers from witnessing the premier event that was about to unfold.

Holding up the garter belt, we noticed in horror that two dangling straps were missing – both on the same leg. Panicked, we bolted from the bathroom and scampered around looking for the missing straps. After a few minutes we noticed Allan, sitting in his room, experimenting with them. He was popping the floor, making a thwacking noise. Kat grabbed the straps from Allan's small hands and marched back to the bathroom. We examined the damaged garment and realized the wet girdle was Kat's only choice. It seemed forever before Kat stopped twisting and turning, fighting the girdle.

Exasperated, she exclaimed, "It's just too small. It won't fit me. I can't get it on."

Stuffing herself into the starch-stiff garment that Mama had purchased just days before for this very moment, Kat mumbled words that I couldn't understand. She continued pulling and twisting, the struggle seemingly more like a wrestling match to me than someone getting dressed as I watched, amazed at her antics. Stifling the desire to laugh, I couldn't believe that the wet garment seemed to have shrunk and that something so small could be stretched over Kat's bony hips.

Finally, she managed to get the wet girdle in place. Panting and in pain, Kat groused, "This ol' thing is so tight I can't breathe. Becomin' a lady won't happen overnight."

I felt the same way but refrained from commenting. It was well enough to let that comment alone. Besides, my thoughts were as Kat would say, *It'll never happen! Not in a million years!*

Kat looked pensive at the tattered stockings and quickly discarded the idea of wearing the bloody garments, pleased, also, that she wouldn't have to shave her legs. Unable to bend at the waist and miserable, she steadied herself by holding onto the towel rack and ordered me to use the shoehorn and put the left shoe on her foot. I crammed her over-sized foot into one of the heels. Now, as I struggled to remove the shoehorn, we realized it had become hopelessly stuck. Kat pulled on the shoehorn while I tugged backwards holding the heel of the shoe, trying to loosen its hold on her foot. After extended effort, the shoehorn dislodged, along with the shoe. I went flying backward, hit the wall hard, slid and landed with a thump on the floor in front of Kat. Shaking my head to clear my thoughts, I wondered if Kat would ever get those heels on her feet. Without a word I just stared at her and with a knowing look between us, we realized this would never work. Looking into each other's eyes, we recognized the hopelessness of the situation.

A slight smile touched Kat's lips as she blurted out an order, "Find those scissors Mama uses to cut our bangs with. I've gotta idea."

"What are you gonna do with 'em?" I asked.

"Just find 'em and I'll show you," Kat retorted.

Picking through the iodine, bandages, rubbing alcohol and peroxide in the medicine cabinet, I couldn't find the scissors. Kat stood on the toilet, opened Mama's makeup drawer, sifted through rouge, lipstick and mascara in an effort to find the illusive scissors.

"Got 'em," she cried out, jumping from the toilet.

"Now what are you gonna do with 'em?" I asked excitedly.

"Gimme that shoe and I'll show you what I'm gonna do," Kat directed.

I reached into the tub, pulled out a high heel and handed it to Kat, wondering what she had in mind. She seemed to be examining the shoe from all sides, trying to make a decision.

Again, I asked, "What are you gonna do?"

"I'm 'bout to show you, just watch," she answered confidently as she plopped on the toilet seat with heel and scissors.

Kat braced the shoe between her knees and started cutting open the seam at the back, thus allowing ankle room for 'GLIDING'.

With a sharp breath, I gasped, "You can't do that!"

"Oh, yeah? Just watch me."

And I did, but was not believing what I was seeing. She continued to manipulate our Mama's old shoes. She actually cut the back off each heel, first one then the other. Next she studied the problem of getting her toes into the narrow space.

"I need more room for my toes," she muttered and hacked away.

She stabbed and carved first the left shoe, then the right, cutting away the offending parts. I watched dumbfounded.

"Now this is more like it. This ol' heel kinda looks like our skates, doesn't it?" Kat mumbled softly, wondering how to improve on the adjustments. "If I could just put wheels on these things and adjust the length with a key, I'd have 'em perfect for my feet."

She turned the shoe over in her hands, considering the possibilities of modifying it into a skate style. She shook her head vigorously and threw the shoe to the floor, dismissing the idea.

Troubling thoughts reeled through my mind and I voiced my fears to Kat, "Look what you've done to Mama's shoes. She isn't gonna like what you did and we're gonna be in a lot of trouble when she sees 'em."

Kat snapped, "Well, she's not gonna find 'em." And with a warning look, said, "Pick up the scraps and flush 'em down the toilet. Don't leave any pieces behind for Mama to see."

Tacitly, as if joining her conspiracy, I asked excitedly, "Where do you think we can hide 'em from Mama?"

"I don't know yet. We'll have to figure that out later. I have to practice now," Kat said, throwing the scissors back into the drawer.

After much ado, Kat was ready to get started. Nagging her into submission, I finally convinced her to wear the stockings, so the heels would slip on easier. Cautiously, Kat slipped her feet into the stockings but refused to pull the nasty things past her ankles.

"I'm not wearin' those things. Get the scissors out again," Kat demanded.

"What for?" I questioned, a bit puzzled.

"Just do it. I'll show you what for," she replied, removing the nylons.

Taking the scissors, she ordered, "You hold the bloody end and I'll hold the toes. Now stretch 'em as far as you can while I cut 'em."

With that settled, she cut each stocking just above the ankle until they separated from the legs. "Throw the rest away," she directed.

I turned to discard the useless hosiery in the trash can, but Kat seized my arm.

"Throw 'em out the window," she ordered. "We'll get 'em later and throw 'em in the woods. We don't want Mama to find 'em in the trash can."

Following orders, I tossed the nasty nylons out the window and returned my attention to the task at hand – getting the shoes on Kat's feet. Still finding it difficult to cram over-sized feet into under-sized shoes, Kat opened the bathroom door and pitched the newly-fashioned heels into the hallway.

Allan scrambled to snatch up the heels ahead of Kat and blurted out, "Watch me do it, Kat. Then you can copy me."

He slid his small feet easily into the heels and pranced down the hallway as we all gawked in amazement. Watching him closely, we hoped to learn a thing or two about gliding from our younger brother.

"See? It's easy! Try it," Allan urged, hoping to help Kat out.

He made it look so incredibly easy that Kat decided to mimic him. She retrieved the heels from Allan and, once again, forced her feet into the heels. Putting the shoes on now tender feet was still difficult, but the sawed-off stockings did help. With fragments of mutilated stockings hanging from her ankles, she was a sight to behold as she stood to take a first tentative step in chopped-up heels and cut off nylons.

Optimistic, Kat announced, "OK, let's get started. If Allan can do it, so can I."

With all the adjustments made, Kat was surprised that the high heel shoes still felt as though they were permanently attached to her feet, and it certainly looked that way to me with her unnaturally arched insteps.

"OUCH!" she kept repeating in misery, pain written all over her face.

With all the agony she was going through there was nothing about becoming a lady that appealed to Kat, especially at that moment. It all seemed impossible that she would ever learn to walk like a lady.

Adding to the impossible situation, Kat was hopelessly pigeon-toed. Her toes were hanging over the cut-out portion of the shoes, trying to escape the confines of their leather prison. I laughed despite myself when I saw her big toes touch each other at an awkward angle as a result of her natural pigeon-toed stance. Her balance at this moment was, at best, precarious. With the first step, her ankles turned askew, causing her to fall to her knees.

"Ouch!" she cried. "How do other girls do this?"

Glaring at me, her look mutely accused me of getting her into this present state of misery. Grabbing me roughly for support, she slowly stood, teetering on the brink of imbalance, painstakingly striving to remain upright. I placed the encyclopedia on her head then rapidly retreated. Trying to imitate Allan, with shoulders hitched up around her ears and arms fluttering like wings for balance, Kat attempted to walk the hall. Second step into the routine, all she succeeded in doing was to have the heavy book slide off her head and crash to the floor. Kat suffered the same fate as I had before, joining the book. Sprawled on top of the encyclopedia, she was a picture of utter defeat. Grim faced, she grabbed the book and got up, determined to start over again. Kat took a tentative step, struggling to remember everything she had to do in order to 'walk like a lady'.

With arms stretched parallel to the floor and hands groping for something to hold onto, Kat again stumbled. The enormity of Kat successfully learning how to walk was apparent to everyone. But even while sympathizing with her, I couldn't control my laughter.

I secretly wondered, *If taking just one step was this much trouble, how was she ever going to glide down the entire length of the hall and back? And how in the world was she going to get across the stage, down the stairs and back to her chair at graduation without stumbling?*

Kat slowly walked down the hall, clutching the book on top of her head. Compared to her, my performance was like a recently crowned Miss America striding confidently down the runway. And, I, having just completed my first walking lesson, and now experienced in gliding, offered to give Kat some valuable pointers. From my view, numerous problems existed.

With every step Kat took, I was eager to give advice. "The problem is you cut the stockings off and you're stumblin' over them. Quit walkin' pigeon-toed. Remember to point your feet out. Balance the book on your head, don't hold it. You're slumpin', so hold your shoulders up. Stop lookin' at your feet and keep your chin up. If you'd listen to me you'd get it right."

Kat paused to catch her breath and glared scornfully at me. Knowing this was my cue to shut up, I backed off and let Kat go it alone. She had at least twenty more steps to take before reaching the end of the hall. Crouched in one corner of the long hallway with my brothers and sister, we watched and cheered her on. Kat clomped her way through the hall in ten giant steps.

"Not bad," announced Kat, losing her balance and falling to one knee as she turned to face us. Catching her breath and elated with her progress, she bragged, "I did good, huh? That was really good, wasn't it?"

Shaking my head in strong disagreement, I thought, *She'll never be able to walk across that stage. I'll have to do it for her, somehow.*

Unable to stand, the exhausted Kat crawled back to her audience of four, collapsed and panted the words, "That's enough for today. Get this stuff off of me so we can go out and play." She fished for compliments on her gliding performance, reminding us. "But, I did real good, huh?"

But having kept count of the things Kat did wrong, big brother Bill blurted the errors for everyone to hear, "The encyclopedia fell off with every other step, you walked pigeon-toed with every step, you fell five times, your shoulders were scrunched up the whole time, and there was certainly no GLIDING going on. You looked like a big ol' bird tryin' to take flight."

Pointing and laughing at her, Allan, even at his age, knew Mama was wasting her time trying to turn Kat into a lady. Our younger sister, Kirk, simply couldn't believe what she had just witnessed and openly wondered if two months would be enough time to teach Kat how to walk properly.

Kat totally ignored them, continuing to be pleased with her progress. While we struggled to pry off the heels and remove the girdle, Kat pronounced, "Bring on the graduation procession." And pointing a finger at each of us, added, "Don't dare tell Mama what we did to her shoes, or else."

No one chAllanged the "or else."

And so it went day after day for several weeks – until Mama wanted to monitor our progress. We had hoped this day would never come, but planned for it just in case it did. After carving up Mama's heels, Kat came up with a scheme to fall back on in case Mama asked for a live performance.

One evening at supper, two weeks into High Heel Boot Camp, Mama announced the dreaded news, "I want to see how you girls are coming along with walking in heels. After supper I want both of you to practice in front of me."

Kirk and the boys had known all along our misdeeds would eventually catch up with us. Now they wondered, since payday had arrived, how Kat and I would extract ourselves from this dilemma. Having made a pact of silence with us, they dared not spill the beans about the ripped up shoes or they would be equally in trouble.

Apparently attempting to smooth over any problems with our training, Bill teasingly exclaimed, "They're doin' great. Wait 'till you see how good they walk in your heels!"

We glared at him a less than subtle warning to say no more. Taking the cue, he grinned sheepishly while looking straight into Mama's eyes.

Suspicious, Mama pointed a forefinger at Bill, "Have you been watching them walk?"

"Oh, yes, Ma'am, we all watch 'em. They practice every day down the hall. They're gettin' real good," Bill answered somewhat snidely.

Our appetites lost and our stomachs nervous, we picked at our food, too upset even to eat a piece of the pineapple upside down cake Mama had prepared for dessert. She thought we were sick. We were, but not with fever as she believed, but more seriously with fear!

Excusing us from the table, Mama directed us to get dressed while everyone else cleaned the dinner dishes, swept the kitchen floor and wiped down the counter tops. As we walked away from the table, cool as cucumbers, we gave no hint that there was anything wrong. Out of Mama's sight, we rushed down the long hallway to the back of the house, stopping only when we reached Mama's room. Opening her closet door, Kat retrieved another old pair of black patent leather high heel shoes stashed in the corner of the closet weeks ago, along with a pair of old stockings stuffed into each toe.

With at least thirty minutes to prepare before the kitchen would be clean, we hurried to the bathroom to bathe and to shave our legs. Finished with these tasks, we dashed to our bedroom and prepared for our work out.

"You go first," Kat ordered.

Resigned to my fate, I struggled into the girdle, donned the garter belt and shimmied into the nylons with exceptional ease. Getting into petticoats and dresses, we studied the heels, dreading the next step.

Kat questioned, "Are you gonna put those on now? I wouldn't. I'd wait 'til Mama is ready."

I responded, "That's a good idea. Help me get 'em on when she calls."

Mama finally summoned, "OK, girls, let's see what you have learned. We want to see you walk."

We looked into each other's eyes for encouragement, hoping we could pull the test off. Legs hanging over the edge of the top bunk, I held my breath and tried, with little success, to shove my feet as hard as I could into the miserable heels. At the other end of the shoe, Kat struggled to shove the too-small shoes onto my feet. At last with the aid of the shoehorn, the shoes finally slid on. In excruciating pain, I pondered how to lower myself to the floor without breaking my ankles. Jumping wasn't an option. Turning around and backing up to the bunk bed, Kat prompted me to ease onto her back when she was in place. I slid easily from her back to the floor. Pain shot through my legs, crippling me momentarily. When the worst of the pain subsided, I began the long walk down the hall to the living room.

Not wanting to miss any of the excitement, our curious siblings greeted us as they sat on the floor in front of Mama and Daddy, eager to see what shoes we were wearing. Judging by the shock on their faces, they were surprised to see two whole shoes instead of the carved ones. Standing behind me, Kat carefully placed the encyclopedia on my head, pushing me forward to begin gliding. Teetering on the brink of imbalance, I regained my composure and held the book atop my head. Closely watching the progress, Mama made no comment. I walked to the fireplace, about five giant steps away, without incident. But when I turned to backtrack, the reference book fell noisily to the floor. There in full view of Mama, I stood rigid, praying she had seen enough.

Her stifled laugh shouted volumes, and smiling, she directed, "Take those shoes off. They're too little. I'll borrow a pair from a friend with bigger feet so you can continue practicing until I buy your new shoes closer to graduation day."

"Hallelujah!" Kat exclaimed, grinning at Mama.

Immediately I sat down on the floor in front of Mama and Daddy and tugged at the offending shoes, finding them stuck to my feet. Looking up at Daddy with imploring eyes, I knew he would aid in removing the bedeviled heels. As I lay on my back with my feet in Daddy's lap, Mama saw I was wearing both the girdle and the damaged garter belt.

She threw both hands out in exasperation and exclaimed, "I told you girls weeks ago to wear one or the other. Not both. If you girls would listen more closely, things would be much easier."

Kat blurted at me, "I told you Mama said to wear just one of these things at a time. But no! You wouldn't listen to me. You had to go and put both of 'em on."

Accepting our admonishment from Mama, we retreated to our bedroom and shut the door before Kirk, Allan or Bill could invade our privacy.

Kat's only comment was, "It always pays for you to go first. That was easy, wasn't it?" Relieved, we felt confident we could conquer High Heel Boot Camp and GLIDE with the best of them in heels that fit our feet. At this point we had everything figured out except how to support Volume A.

Sitting together giggling on the lower bunk bed, we chanted in unison, "Shoulders up, stomach in, chin out, head high, feet straight and GLIDE," over and over with emphasis on the last word.

A few days before graduation, on a return trip to Neilson's Department Store, Mama directed the attendant, "Please check their sizes and bring out two pair of white patent leather shoes." Eying me, then turning to Kat, Mama added, "I don't think you girls are ready for heels or even pumps, so we're going to buy some regular Sunday shoes."

We looked at Mama, astonished at this announcement and glad that we would be donning comfortable shoes.

"It'll be easy to glide in those shoes," Kat exclaimed with a big grin on her face. "Can't wait to get home and start practicin'," she continued as she kicked the wad of tissue that had been stuffed in the shoe across the department floor.

We did graduate the sixth grade and succeeded in walking across the stage without too many mishaps. Kat accepted her diploma and with long strides waited for me at the steps leading off the auditorium. I, of course, glided perfectly, receiving the diploma with dignity. As I caught up with Kat, we donned huge smiles, knowing that we had pulled it off. Going down the steps of the stage, Kat tripped over her feet and fell backward into me. We recovered nicely as we stumbled down the rest of the steps, landed on our feet and strolled unabashed back to our seats, grinning from ear to ear that we had accomplished our goal without embarrassing anyone.

Mama never was successful in getting Kat to glide, and the encyclopedia trick was lost on her. To this day, Kat is more comfortable in tennis shoes and socks. As a matter of fact, she doesn't even own a pair of panty hose or a pair or high-heels, and certainly not a girdle or garter belt. It'll never happen, not in a million years.

THE LONG WALK HOME

When we were in sixth grade, Kat and I were responsible for walking our little sister, Kirk, and her classmate, Ricky Jones, safely home from school. Kirk and Ricky were third graders who needed older, wiser, and more experienced walkers to step off the mile-long trek from just west of the Square to our home on Park Drive.

We were cautioned not to talk to strangers and never to accept a ride home with anyone we didn't know. These instructions must have been standard from all parents. We knew practically everyone in our small town and always felt safe, only occasionally encountering a stranger. However, we listened to our parents and were always on the lookout for that "stranger" who might approach us.

Before our older brother, Bill, entered the seventh grade at University High School on the Ole Miss campus, he was the one charged with seeing that we younger children got home safely. Sometimes though, we still waited for Bill to walk the half mile from UHS to meet us on the schoolhouse steps before striking out for home. But on most afternoons Kat and I herded our young troops homeward by ourselves. The few minutes of fidgeting, waiting for Bill seemed like a lifetime wasted – time that we could spend playing in our yard. So we'd usually strike out on our own.

As the yellow buses pulled away from the red-faced school building, the candy store across the street beckoned to us. Hurrying to this child's paradise, we would stare longingly at the wonderful array of sugary treats, trying to decide whether to spend our carefully hoarded pennies on bubble gum, dots, jaw breakers, taffy, tootsie roll pops, or sugar Daddydies. Often we would spend our time inside Mistillis' eyeing the display of candy and wishing we had more money to spend. Every cent saved was spent on all the candy our meager funds could buy. Often we pooled our money, with Ricky throwing in his few pennies, in order to buy a bigger bag of candy for all to share. After making our purchases, we would dole out the goodies evenly and take our time eating the candy to make it last while waiting for Bill. On the days that our pockets were empty, we reluctantly headed home, not wanting to waste time waiting for him.

When Bill was with us, our group of five, ages eight to twelve, made the long walk home with few interferences from outside. As the old adage goes, we found safety in numbers. We needed mass numbers because there were kids along the way who would too often try to pick a fight. The mere presence of Kat and Bill was an effective deterrent to anyone having the nerve to start something. On the days when Bill didn't accompany us, Kat alone was sufficiently intimidating to prevent trouble from any bully. They just were not brave enough to mess with her.

One spring morning in April, 1960, Kat awoke with a stomach ache and begged to stay home from school. Mama always confirmed our claims of illness with a thermometer because she believed if we had fever we were indeed sick. Before the thermometer had time to register her temperature, Kat sprang from the bed and reached the toilet just in time. Mama shook her head, realizing Kat really was sick and not just pretending as she had tried to do on other occasions in the past.

With Kat sick and having to stay home from school, I turned to Bill for reassurance that he would accompany us home that day after school. Shock registered on my face when he told me he would be staying after school to finish a science project. Then full comprehension hit me hard when I realized I was responsible for getting us home from school safely. For you see, the day before on the playground at recess, Kat had been confronted by the school bully, a kid called Junior. He had bragged to everyone within ear shot about his new marbles. He was especially proud of his red and green cat-eye shooter. Hearing the word marbles and interested in a new shooter, Kat turned to see who was talking and found herself face to face with Junior. Making casual conversation, Kat said politely, "I like to shoot marbles, do you?"

With a gleam in his eye Junior responded with his own question, "Do you wanna play a game?"

Kat was quick to ask, "For keeps?"

"Yeah, for keeps. Why else do you play marbles?" he snorted.

Unfazed by his attitude, Kat chAllanged. "I'll see you at recess in front of the swings."

When the morning recess bell rang, we ran out to the playground, racing for the swings. Kat sauntered into the woods behind the swings, picked up a stick and returned to where I stood. She drew a three foot diameter circle in the sand, tossed the stick aside and waited for Junior to appear.

Within minutes he swaggered, self-assured, to the rim of the circle, bringing with him a gang of onlookers who were convinced of the outcome before the first marble hit the ground. It was as if an imaginary line had been drawn in the sand straight through the diameter of the circle. This created two semi-circles with Junior's band of buddies on one side of the line. Supporting Junior in his quest for victory were three of our classmates, Roger Tubbs, Bill Bryant and John Tubbs, along with a bunch of Junior's fifth grade cronies. Standing two and three deep, they strained to get a look at the two contestants.

Taking up allegiance around the other half circle in a face-off with the boys was Kat's support group. I could hear Wanda Boatright, Donna Ptak and Brenda Faust voicing their cheers for Kat. Denny Keye stood next to me whispering in my ear a chant for all the girls to sing once Kat had won.

Kat hovered over the circle with a fist full of marbles and insisted as she released her prized cat eyes into the circle, "Drop your marbles, Junior. You shoot first."

Junior replied insultingly, "Naw. Sissy girls go first."

That concession was exactly what Kat wanted. She grinned broadly and quickly agreed, "OK."

Kat crouched on her knees, poised with the larger shooter marble in the knuckle down position at the arc of the circle and lined up her first target – the marble closest to the rim. "I think I'll go for that yella one," she mumbled.

The school bully noticed Kat setting aim for his favorite marble and laughingly taunted, "I betcha can't even come close to hittin' that one."

Kat looked up at Junior, noted his support group jeering at her, and then concentrated on aiming and released her shooter. It hit dead on, rolling the yellow agate out of the circle.

She gloated, "That yella one's mine, Margaret. Pick it up for me, will ya?"

I dusted it off and stuck it in my pocket, waiting for the next shot, whispering in Kat's ear, "Get the red one next."

Junior blurted, eyes blazing "Lucky shot. Betcha can't do that again."

Kat responded tersely, "Just watch me," as she stepped into the circle, picked up her shooter, knuckled down again and blasted Junior's second marble from the circle.

Kat looked up and smiled maliciously at Junior and his buddies as she tucked her skirt behind her knees and knelt to shoot again, repeating his line, "Yeah. Pretty lucky, huh?"

Eyeing Junior's closest marble, a solid blue agate, Kat punched it through the circle and homed in on the next target, a blue and white cat eye. Kat hit the marble but failed to hit it out, leaving her shooter marble exposed. She reluctantly stepped out of the circle, relinquishing it to Junior, who sidled up to the rim, squatted and took aim.

Before releasing his shooter, Junior grinned up at his buddies and bragged, "This is gonna be easy. Just watch me take the rest of these, boys."

As Kat and I stood together looking at a possible disaster, she whispered, "If he gets my shooter, the game's over. He gets all of the marbles, even the ones I've already won."

Denny stepped up beside Kat, looked down at Junior and blurted out, "Betcha can't hit it," over and over again. The chant caught on and soon all the girls were singing the tune, unnerving the school bully.

Junior knuckled down at the rim of the circle, aiming for Kat's shooter with Denny's mantra ringing in his ears. His cheering squad urged him on, giving him a false sense of confidence, which proved to be his downfall.

Kat whispered softly in my ear, "Look how Junior's holdin' his marble. He's not doin' it right. His knuckle isn't in the right place. It hasta be squared to the ground. He'll never hit it out. You just watch and see."

Suspense hung in the air as the onlookers held their breath waiting for the shot. I watched Junior's shooting hand, spellbound as the marble was released. It rolled quickly at first as it left his fingers but slowed down considerably when it finally nudged Kat's shooter, leaving them an inch apart inside the circle.

The girls began jumping and down shouting a new chant, "Kat's gonna win! Kat's gonna win!"

The boys, heads bowed, were moaning their disappointment, anticipating Junior's fate.

Jumping up and down, Denny taunted, singing, "You didn't hit it. You didn't hit it. I told you so. I told you so." She continued, "Everybody knows Kat's the best at marbles. Everybody 'cept you."

The crowd fell silent as Kat deliberately stepped into the circle confidently claiming, "My turn."

I whispered to Denny beaming, "Kat's not gonna make the same mistake ol' Junior did. She'll blast that marble and show him up."

Crouched on her left knee, Kat took aim and, in less than a second, Junior's shooter rolled from the circle. Within arm's length, she grabbed the ousted shooter and the remaining marbles, stood up and claimed victory, holding the marbles out for her elated support group and Junior's dejected buddies to see.

Junior's boys displayed quite the opposite reaction, jeering at him as they sauntered away. Several even complained, "I can't believe you let a girl beat you. I thought you were better than that."

Embarrassed but angrier at Kat's celebration, Junior vowed, "I'll get my marbles back. You wait and see."

Shaking both fists full of marbles in Junior's face, Kat retorted, "You made the rules and these are mine now. Game's over. Winner's keepers, loser's weepers."

Desperate to get his marbles back, Junior threatened, "I'll get you back for this. Just wait."

Backing into the remaining gawkers, Junior faced Kat with a sneer on his face, the look of someone who smelled sauerkraut cooking. A determined Kat stared him down with the promise they could settle it here and now. With the marbles clinched in her fist, she was ready to punch his lights out. Mumbling inaudibly under his breath, Junior slunk away, defeated. After all, he was just a little fifth grader and no match for Kat. But even so, I was afraid of him. After all, he was the school bully and didn't know me from Kat.

To make matters worse, as the bell rang for recess to end, Kat saw Junior running for the water line and, determined to beat him, caught up from behind and slid easily in line ahead of him. When he arrived a few seconds later, Kat laughed, "Girls can run, too." And, adding to his chagrin, Kat showed everyone in line her new marbles.

Denny announced for all to hear, "Kat beat Junior at marbles. You shoulda seen her take his shooter and the rest of 'em. Man, she was good."

Fuming, an angry Junior repeated his promise, spitting out the words one by one, "I'll get my marbles back, you sissy girl. I'll get my marbles back. You wait and see."

Back in the classroom, word of Kat's victory quickly spread, and before class resumed, she passed the newly acquired marbles around for everyone to inspect. I began fidgeting and worrying about Junior's threat, voicing my concerns to Kat.

I whined, "What are we gonna do 'bout Junior? He's a bully and will beat us up."

Kat firmly replied, "Don't worry 'bout him. He's just a fifth grader. He can't hurt us. Just stay away from him the rest of the day."

I settled into my desk behind Kat and leaned into her back whispering, "But we have to walk by his street on our way home from school. What if he stops us and tries to beat us up?"

Kat turned around and faced me, responding to my concerns, "He won't beat you up as long as I'm around. Now stop worryin'."

Kat's reassuring words combined with Junior's recent threats were playing over and over in my mind as I now stood, twenty-one hours later, beside Kat's sick bed listening to a well-devised plan to circumvent any ensuing problems I might encounter after school.

During the school day, both recesses were absent any confrontation since Junior seemed resigned to stay away from me, and I certainly didn't go looking for him. As I thought over the plan and tried to perfect it throughout the day, I was nevertheless apprehensive about running into Junior. He lived between the school and the graveyard along the only path we were allowed to walk home each day. I was mortally afraid of Junior, and though neither Bill nor Kat seemed the least bit intimidated by him, the frightening thought of standing alone before him made me want to cry. In order for our plan to work, I would have to keep my emotions in check – no crying!

As the end of the school day approached and the last bell rang for us to be dismissed, I anxiously awaited Kirk and Ricky's arrival at the front steps of the school for the long walk home. When they finally arrived, I told them of the plan that Kat and I had conjured up earlier that day. They agreed that we could pull it off, relieving me of any doubt that it would work. As we walked home, we practiced what we'd say if Junior appeared in our path. Their belief in the plan gave me confidence not felt before.

As we casually strolled down the steps on our way from school and ambled slowly down Jefferson Avenue toward the cemetery, we looked carefully down each side street for Junior before hurrying across to safety. We continued rehearsing our lines, knowing that success depended on all of us doing and saying the right things at the right time. As we rounded the corner of Jefferson Avenue and Avent Street with no bully in sight, our spirits brightened. We were past the street where he lived and hoped we were home free. Even though I was relieved that a confrontation had been averted, Kirk and Ricky were disappointed that the lines we had so diligently practiced wouldn't be needed after all. Convinced that we could always use this plan if necessary in the future, we agreed not to tell anyone about the details of the plan, lest it be ruined.

Ricky quickly crossed the street to the ornate fence that surrounded St. Peter's Cemetery to grab a light green and bumby bodock from the edge of the street. He quickly kicked it soccer style to me and Kirk on the side of the street opposite the cemetery. I always walked across the street from the graveyard, reluctant to get too close to whoever was in there. As the overcast skies began to rumble and the breeze sprinkled rain on our faces, we ran laughing homeward, abandoning the bodock and any thoughts of a confrontation. At the bottom of the hill, just past the fence line, a figure jumped from behind a tree as a clap of thunder erupted from the sky. We screamed in unison as the figure closed in on us, pushing us backward into the cemetery fence. With effort, we managed to gather our wits as we realized who had scared us. Angry at being frightened by this bully, I stepped in front of Kirk and Ricky, keeping them behind me. I reached into my pockets and pulled out two hands full of marbles, ready to punch Junior in the face.

Hearing the marbles clank against each other, Junior shouted over the thunder, "Are those my marbles? Give 'em to me!"

I retorted with more confidence than I felt, "These are my marbles. Remember? Winners keepers, losers weepers? I won! You lost! And I'm ready to give 'em to you in your face."

Ricky and Kirk chimed in with their well-rehearsed lines, "Go get him, Kat. Beat him up, Kat. You can beat up anybody, Kat. Go ahead and hit him, Kat."

Junior, now unsure and not so cocky, stepped backward at the sound of Kat's name. Moving away from the others, I purposely strode directly toward the bully, faking bravado I really didn't feel. Then with Ricky's last, "Get him, Kat," I surged forward as if to pounce on him.

Suddenly, Junior spun about and scurried up the slippery slope to St. Peters Cemetery. As I closed menacingly in on him, he slipped and tumbled to the bottom of the hill. Looking over his shoulder and seeing how close I was, he scampered quickly up the hill again on all fours. At the top finally, he turned to stare wild-eyed down at us.

We were laughing and yelling, "Look at the yella-belly chicken," with clucking sounds to accompany the jeering.

The last we saw of Junior, he was speeding pell-mell through the cemetery, dodging headstones as he slipped and fell on the wet ground in an effort to escape.

Without a second thought, we ran as fast as we could to the safety of Ricky's house on Williams Street. Holding hands in an effort to keep the slowest runner from lagging, we crowded breathlessly onto the small front porch stoop out of the pouring rain. Searching left and right for any return of the cowardly bully, Kirk and I left Ricky's house, taking an indirect route home through Avent Park, vigilant to keep an eye peeled for Junior's possible retaliation.

Bursting through the front door wringing wet, Kirk and I toweled off as we told Kat the story of our adventure. Between gasps of air and both of us talking at once, we related every detail of how scared we had been when Junior jumped out at us from behind the cemetery tree.

Kat requested, "Tell me again how you made him run away."

I repeated, "The plan, it worked. Kirk and Ricky kept blurtin' out your name and the more they called me Kat the more scareder Junior got. So he just ran for it when I started after him. You shoulda seen him rollin' down that hill when he slipped. You shoulda seen him crawlin' back up that hill and runnin' for it. We saw him hidin' behind tombstones lookin' back at us before runnin' to the next one."

Smiling with delight, Kat mused, "We won't have to worry about Junior any more. That ol' fifth grader got what was comin' to him. And you were the one who scared him off. I wish I coulda been there. Tell it to me again. I wanna hear it all over again."

FINICKY EATERS

When we were youngsters there were both advantages and disadvantages being identical twins. While most people considered us one unit – The King Twins – we were determined to have our own identities, with a few exceptions. Avoidance of eating disgusting food was one of those exceptions. It was an uphill battle, especially at dinnertime, so we united as co-conspirators in our attempts to dispose of unwanted food. It pitted us – Margaret and me – against them, Mama and her cooking.

We gave new meaning to the term FINICKY EATERS. There were two tests that every food we ate had to pass – the smell test and the eyeball test.

When smelly odors drifted down the hall from the kitchen, Margaret often commented as she waved the bedroom door frantically back and forth to air out the room, "I'm not eating that ol' stuff. It stinks." With her nose scrunched and lips pursed, she proclaimed it yuck. "Pee-yew," she'd say. "What in the world is Mama cookin'?"

The food had to look good and smell good in order for us to even consider putting it in our mouths. In this pact we did not waver, we were as one.

On the other hand, when wonderful smelling aromas wafted back to our bedroom, we looked forward to a scrumptious meal of possibly eating tons of French fries. The letdown came when we entered the kitchen only to find something such as fried oysters plopped on a paper towel draining excess grease. Fried oysters were considered a special meal around our house, but to look at an oyster before it was prepared disgusted us.

I remarked to Margaret the first time oysters appeared on the menu in the summer of 1960, when we were twelve years old, "Do you remember what those things looked like when Mama dumped 'em into the cornmeal batter?"

"Yeah," Margaret responded, adding, "It's disgustin'. We gotta eat the head, guts, brains and all. It makes me wanna gag."

Not wanting to be left out, I added, "Makes you wanna puke, too. Those ugly things would gag a buzzard!"

Some nights were like that. On those nights when we didn't know what was being prepared for dinner, we still had to figure out how NOT to eat it – just in case.

When Mama prepared meals for our family of seven, she was rightfully exasperated when it didn't meet everyone's approval. We often turned our noses up at the food she spent hours cooking, and Mama grew immeasurably frustrated with our attitudes. She was determined that we were going to at least sample everything she had prepared. But we were equally determined not to. In a battle of strong wills, Mama always thought she won, but we knew better. We had other plans in the works, and we learned quickly to hide our disapproval of all disgusting foods while in her presence. More importantly, we knew how to get rid of items on our plates without eating them and without getting caught. Some foods were much easier to dispose of than others. Casseroles were messy, heavy and difficult to hide. On the other hand, food like English peas were a cinch to get rid of since they easily rolled off the rim of the plate onto the table and into our laps. Never to be outdone, we mastered the art of making any food vanish as the two of us worked our strategies prior to each evening meal.

During the summer of '60, Daddy grew a large garden down by the creek that flowed along the bottom of the hill behind our house. We were charged with gathering vegetables from the garden. Earlier in the spring he planted a variety of vegetables – some to our liking, but most were not at all pleasing to our palates. Corn and potatoes met our approval. All the rest of the garden – purple-hull peas, greens, cabbage, butter beans, string beans, carrots, okra and peppers – were on the not-to-be-eaten-at-all-cost list. When we gathered the vegetables each day, we knew they would likely be the very ones on our plates at the evening meal. In order to escape having to eat these undesirable foods, we plotted while we picked and carried the buckets full of vegetables up the steep hill to the house. Our ultimate goal at the beginning of supper was to get to the desserts. In order to accomplish this, we had to eat everything Mama placed on our plates. This was a tremendous chAllange for us since we turned our noses up at most of the food she put before us. Evening meals consisted of a meat, several vegetables, bread and dessert. We were bread and dessert girls. Sometimes we approved of the meat, but hardly ever the vegetables.

One hot muggy evening in August when we came in from play, the initial cooking smells were already drifting from the kitchen. Way too often, we thought, those odors smelled as though they came from the bathroom; but, in fact, it was only collards cooking. Not even Popeye the Sailor Man could convince us to eat spinach. We didn't even want to sample it. Thus, we yet again put our Plan 1, which was the no-gross-food-will-pass-our-lips plan, into action. Mama's plan was that we had to eat a portion of every new recipe that she prepared. Even if it were only a single bite – we had to try it or no dessert. This was just one of the unbreakable mealtime rules around the King house. The two meal plans - ours and Mama's - clashed.

That night, after going into the bathroom to wash up before supper, Margaret closed the door behind us in an attempt to shut out the disgusting smells. She pinched her nose, and then asked, "Do you smell that? What is it? I'm not eatin' that stuff!"

"What could we be havin' that stinks so bad?"

"She must be cookin' that squash with onions that we picked this mornin'. How can anybody eat food that smells that bad?" Margaret groused.

Reluctantly, I volunteered, "Let me sneak thru the livin' room and peek into the kitchen to see what's on the stove."

"Okay. But hurry up. We don't have much time to figure this one out," Margaret cautioned.

"I have to wait 'til Mama crosses to the sink. When I hear the water runnin' I can peek into the kitchen."

I tiptoed around the living room furniture, then with my back to the wall slid silently to the open doorway. With the wall as a shield, I crept to within inches of the stove, and waited patiently for what seemed to be an eternity. Mama lifted the pot lid and foul odors drifted my way, deadening my sense of smell. Stifling a cough, I covered my nose and mouth. I finally heard the tap water running in the sink, my cue to steal a quick glance at the four pots on the stove top. I looked back and forth from Mama to the pots, fearing I would get caught.

I quickly took inventory of the two pots without lids and made a hasty retreat to Margaret announcing, "It's squash all right. You got that right. But I don't know what that stuff is in the other two pots 'cause they had tops on 'em. It's probably cabbage or spinach. It smelled terrible."

Margaret inquired, "What was in the last pot?"

"I don't know. Some mushy stuff and there was some purple peels on the countertop."

Margaret blurted, "Purple!" We've never had purple food before. Are you sure it's purple?"

I answered emphatically while reaching for the Ivory soap to wash up, "Yeah, it's purple, a kinda pretty dark purple. I've never seen it before."

"Hmm, I guess she'll make us try it," Margaret mused. "But it stinks and I don't wanna taste it. What are we gonna do?"

I quickly agreed, "Yeah it stinks so bad I had to pinch my nose and breathe through my mouth. We gotta do somethin'."

Coming into the dining room, we always found the rectangular chrome table set with six place settings – one for each of the five children and one for Daddy. The limited seating capacity forced Mama to take her meal in the solitude of the den, away from the chattering of five children.

Whispering conspiratorially, we passed by the stove, momentarily holding our breath. Mama looked at us quizzically and questioned, "What are you two girls whispering about? And now you're quiet. Take your seat at the table."

"We're not hungry. Can we just go out and play?" Margaret begged, all the while knowing Mama never relented.

"Absolutely not! You girls sit down and get ready for the blessing."

"Yes, Ma'am," we muttered together as we joined Daddy, Bill, Kirk, and Allan at the table.

With heads bowed, Daddy repeated The King Blessing, "Gracious Lord, forgive our sins, accept our thanks and save our souls, in Christ's name we pray. Amen."

Dishing out a portion from each pot on the stove, Mama handed a plate to Daddy, who relayed it to me. I handed it off to Margaret hoping the next plate would have less food on it. I couldn't believe what was on it.

Looking up at Daddy and pointing to the mush, I asked, "What's that stuff? And what's this slimy stuff comin' out of the top of the okra?"

Overhearing the conversation, Mama replied, "Katherine, the mush is eggplant. I didn't put much on your plate and I expect you to eat every bite. It's good for you. Mind me, now."

"Yes, Ma'am, I will," I said reluctantly.

"But do we have to eat it all? What if we don't like it?" Margaret piped in.

Turning from the stove with another plate of food to dole out, Mama addressed her brood of five, "Now look here. I've spent the last several hours cooking your supper. You'll eat everything I put on your plate or no dessert."

"What's for dessert? I don't see it on the counter," Bill inquired.

"When you finish eating, you'll find out. Now eat your supper, including the okra and eggplant," Mama said stiffly.

Looking at Mama quizzically, we all wondered what eggplant was. Allan, our youngest sibling at six years old, blurted out, "We had eggs for breakfast. They're yella. This doesn't look like eggs. I didn't know eggs came from plants? I don't want any of those green eggs. Do I have to eat 'em?" And then turning to the right, added, "I'm not hungry, Daddy. Can I go out and play?"

Mama retorted, "No! You may not go out and play! What you can do is eat all of your supper. This is my last word on the subject. Eat your supper or no desserts." She just had to add, "There are starving children all around the world who would love to have this food to eat."

With Mama's back turned away from the table we rolled our eyes at each other. We would gladly have given those hungry kids around the world our awful smelling food.

"They must be desperate to want this foul-smellin' stuff," I grumbled to the others out of Mama's ear shot.

We surveyed the plate full of undesirable food, hoping it would go away and knowing it wouldn't. We liked the meat loaf, corn bread and corn on the cob, but the okra, eggplant and squash had to go.

Mama retired to the den to eat in solitude after putting Daddy in charge of keeping track of exactly how much everyone was eating. As she dined alone in peace and quiet, Margaret and I took advantage of the opportunity to dump the offensive food. I nudged Margaret and gave her a subtle signal, tapping my index finger on the edge of the table between our plates, that Plan 1 might work tonight.

Mama's view of the dining room table was such that she could see everyone except Bill and Margaret. She was able to keep constant tabs on me as the meal progressed. Under such a watchful eye, I considered this situation the ultimate chAllange. We were well aware that Mama, while seated in the den, could not see Margaret and we could work this to our advantage. A second problem we had to contend with was being boxed in between the table and the wall, making it impossible for either of us to leave until the meal was finished. Mama had us right where she wanted us. As if these two problems weren't enough to deal with, we also had Daddy sitting immediately to my left, paying more attention to his food than monitoring our plates, yet a concern nonetheless. Distracting Daddy was now as equally important as keeping watch on Mama. This was Margaret's job if Plan 1 was to come together.

Just minutes before we entered the kitchen on the way to the dining room table, we snatched extra napkins and stuffed them into our pockets, knowing we would need them later. Before sitting down at the table, Margaret noted the items left on the counter: salt, pepper, lemon, catsup, and sugar. At just the right time, and timing was everything, we began to activate our strategy. A quick succession of events had to take place, beginning at the precise moment Mama focused on her dinner plate.

I kicked Margaret's leg under the table and she piped up, "Daddy, I need some sugar for my tea. It's bitter."

Daddy scooted his chair back, stood and grabbed the sugar bowl, taking only a few seconds to retrieve the requested item. The second he rose and turned his back on us, I watched for Mama to lower her head to get a bite of food. When all events were synchronized perfectly to our liking, we quickly raked the most offensive food, the eggplant, from our plates into the sturdy napkin spread open on our laps. We repeated this ritual several times during the meal and were able to easily dispose of most of the yucky food on our plates. An unfortunate byproduct of this plan was napkins laden with piles of unwanted food.

Since we ate faster than anyone else at the table, Bill playfully offered, "Want seconds, Kat? Here, I'll get you some more squash and Marg some more boiled okra."

"No, no. I'm full. I don't want anything else 'cept dessert," I blurted before he had time to get out of his chair.

"Nope. I've still got some meatloaf to eat," Margaret replied, picking at the remaining food on her plate. I'm almost done, aren't you?"

"No," Bill responded then added, "I don't seem to eat as fast as you two."

I glanced across the table at Allan eating the last bite of eggplant casserole atop the boiled okra pod. The sour expression on his face reinforced my decision to get rid of it.

Listening to the dining room chatter, the pat question from the den reached our ears as Mama asked, "Travis, did everyone eat their meals?"

Looking around the table to verify his answer, Daddy replied, "Sure did," words we waited to hear in order to be awarded desserts.

We nervously waited for Daddy to finish eating, since he held the key to the disposal of the discarded food in our laps. Directly behind his chair was the trash can, situated in a position that we couldn't get to until he finished his meal. The instant Daddy vacated his chair, a din of noise and confusion allowed Margaret to quickly pass her wad of napkins to me, and I, in turn, in one swift motion, lifted the trashcan lid and dumped the unwanted food, strategically under garbage already in the can. The last thing we needed was for Mama or Daddy to lift the lid of the trashcan and discover our pile of discarded napkins full of our dinner meal.

An additional problem we faced was the "wet spot" left on our shorts once the napkin was dumped, especially where the soggy eggplant casserole or oozing okra had rested! To cover the stain, we grabbed more napkins, unfolded and tucked them at the waist much like Daddy often did, thus covering up the obvious blotch. Silent partners to our schemes were our sister and two brothers who would never have divulged these secrets to our parents. They knew they would someday need our assistance to dispose of their unwanted food. Failure to eat everything on our plates meant no desserts – and getting desserts was the ultimate goal at every meal. Thus, one of our well-thought out plans had to work every time.

The next evening minute steak, mashed potatoes topped with English peas, steamed carrots and cornbread were on the menu. So was chocolate pudding! And to top it all off, dinner preparation was running late.

Mama called, "Katherine, come help me in the kitchen."

I rolled my eyes at Margaret, dreading kitchen duty, and whispered, "Why don't you go. You're better at that cookin' stuff than I am."

"No, she called you, so I guess she wants you to help," Margaret responded.

I clomped my way up the hall to the kitchen. Mama looked up and ordered, "Stir the milk into the cornbread mixture. And be careful you don't spill any of it."

I picked up the wooden spoon and began mixing the ingredients together. As I swirled the milk around the bowl some of the cornmeal splattered onto the counter. I looked up at Mama and shrugged with my shoulders.

Mama shook her head from side to side, reacting to the mess, "Stop being so sloppy. I don't know how in the world you get anything done left-handed. Leave it alone for now. Get over to the sink and wash up those glasses first so I can put tea in them, then when you finish the glasses, I would like for you to wash those bowls I left on the counter over there," she directed, pointing to the countertop behind me.

Picking up the soapy sponge, I washed, rinsed, and dried two glasses before turning my attention to the last one, which slipped from my grasp, shattering in the sink.

Irritated, Mama turned to me, admonishing, "Run get Margaret and tell her to come help me. Go on now. Out of the kitchen before you destroy everything."

I rushed to the back of the house, glad to be out of the kitchen. I told Margaret, "We're havin' minute steak, carrots, English peas, and potatoes for supper."

"It's ready? That was fast," Margaret replied.

"Naw, it's not ready yet. Mama wants you to go help her," I informed Margaret.

She glared at me questioning, "Why? What did you do?"

I answered, "Nothin'. She just wants you. Besides I'm left-handed. And I broke somethin'."

"Margaret, come help me in the kitchen," came the request from Mama shortly.

Hands on hips, Margaret complained, "You always get outta doin' work."

I countered trying to change the subject, "That doesn't matter right now. I've got to figure out how to dump the food from our plates once it's in front of us. Now, go help Mama before she has to call you again. She's waitin' on you."

Fuming, Margaret stomped up the hall, slamming the bedroom door behind her.

Returning to our bedroom thirty minutes later, Margaret announced rather tersely, "Supper's ready. Wash up."

"Wait just a minute," I countered just as tersely. "We gotta decide how to get rid of that tough ol' minute steak. Remember when we had it last time, how tough it was?"

"Yeah, I remember. We chewed and chewed and chewed. Don't know why they call it 'minute steak'. It takes five minutes to chew it up and then you have to swallow it almost whole," Margaret confirmed.

I continued, "It has that hard stuff in it that you can't chew up. I don't like the way it feels in my mouth and I'm not gonna swallow it whole again. So, let's use Plan 2 and I'm gettin' rid of those green peas the same way I did last time. I hate it when Mama messes up my mash potatoes with those things."

Margaret maintained, "I like them on top of the potatoes. They're good that way. You should try it."

"Naw, I don't wanna mess up my mash potatoes. And I don't want the carrots either, so I'm gonna to get rid of them, too."

"Yeah. Good idea. That means both of us hafta grab lots of napkins. But don't let Mama catch us," Margaret cautioned.

Scooting chairs up to the table, we relayed plates of food around the table counterclockwise.

Bill asked the blessing and commented, "Hmmm, this looks delicious, doesn't it, Kat? We really like peas and these little steaks, Mama."

Suspicious at the teasing tone in Bill's voice, Mama raised her eyebrows and stared into each face before announcing, "You will eat this meat and every pea on your plate or no dessert. Understand?" Turning to the stove, she added, "Katherine, that especially goes for you, every pea."

Glaring squint-eyed at Bill, I warned him with my silent stare to shut up and say no more.

Enjoying the moment and the safety of his surroundings, Bill continued sweetly, "We'll eat it all. Daddy is here to watch us."

Not to worry, I thought as I cut the minute steak into five large pieces, preparing it for disposal.

Stacking a carrot slice on top of a piece of meat, I stabbed it with my fork and reluctantly placed it in the center of my mouth. Trying not to grimace or gag with the awful food, I pretended to chew happily as if the food were delicious. Seconds later I took the napkin from my lap and with both hands wiped my mouth, depositing the un-chewed food into it. Four more times and the yucky steak was gone. To my right, Margaret was mirroring my actions until all of the gristly steak was miraculously eaten.

Now, for the peas. I waited until Daddy was distracted with pouring Kirk some more milk. I hurriedly raked the peas over the right side of the plate, rolling them one by one into my napkin. I just finished the pea-disposal task when Mama appeared at the kitchen table ready to inspect our plates.

Astonished and pointing to the floor, Mama fussed, "Allan, how could you possibly make such a mess? Get down there and pick up all those peas."

Puzzled, Allan looked down to see the scattering of peas at his feet, explaining, "I didn't do that. I ate all my peas, see?"

"Yes, you did. You do this every time we have English peas. They must roll off your plate. They're right here on the floor under your chair. Now, hop to it. Pick them up," Mama instructed, patting Allan's rear end as he hopped down.

Margaret and I looked at each other and grinned broadly as Mama placed the chocolate pudding, six bowls and spoons on the table. Mission accomplished.

The next evening Daddy was at a farmer's group meeting, leaving the five of us to dine without him.

With extra space at the table, I scooted around, taking up his post near the garbage can. It was a good thing, too, because we were having string beans, ground beef and corn casserole, and boiled new potatoes. In Daddy's absence we had loaf bread, which Margaret and I loved to eat. But all five of us hated the casserole and dreaded this meal more than most.

As we sat at the table staring at the plates in front of us, Mama directed, "I'm going to be in the den eating my meal. I'll be watching you and I want you to eat every bite." Of course, she had to add, "Or no desserts."

"Yes, Ma'am," we all replied in unison, knowing full well we had no intention of eating most of it.

Bill inquired, "What's for desserts tonight, Mama?"

"A new recipe I tried. I think you'll like it." At those words, we looked at each other wide-eyed, anticipating a scrumptious dessert, wondering what it could be.

As soon as Mama had retreated to the comfort of the den and had settled into her favorite chair, we set to work. I slipped the garbage can top askew, readying it for the bulk of our unwanted food. Once seated, facing me, Mama glanced around the table to ensure we were behaving and eating as she had instructed.

I cleared my throat to initiate the plan. In a soft voice, lips barely moving, ventriloquist style, I told my co-conspirators, "I'm watchin' Mama. When I count to three, scrape some food into your napkin. When I get to three again, pass it to me. Don't dump it all at once. We've got plenty of time. Don't make a mess or Mama will be mad at us. Bill, start talkin' about how high I climbed in the tree today. But not loud, just normal talkin'."

Bill began, "Kat, you climbed nearly to the top of that big ol' tree today. How did you do that?"

I casually responded, "That's easy." I mouthed through clinched teeth and said quietly, "OK on three. One, two, three." We all scraped the most offensive food first.

Margaret chimed in, "Well, I was right behind her, didn't you see me?"

As Mama lowered her head to slice a piece of steak, I broke in and whispered, "On three, pass. One, two, three." The food-ladened napkins were passed to me.

Jumping into the conversation, Allan pleaded, "Help me climb up there, Kat."

"I can't. It's too high for you," I explained.

Pouting, Allan fussed, "No, it's not too high. You can help me."

Getting into my role, I responded, "Stop pesterin' me. I said you're too little." Whispering, I added, "I gotta get rid of this stuff in my lap. Keep talkin'. "

When Mama was focused on her plate of food, I grabbed a bunch of mushy napkins from my lap, reached around the back of my chair and deposited the lumps into the garbage can.

Allan was saying, "This is fun."

Bill kicked Allan and admonished with, "Shhhh."

Mama picked up on the shushing sound and inquired, "What's fun? And why are you trying to keep Allan quiet?"

Bill quickly explained, "Allan thinks climbin' tall trees is fun. He's gettin' loud at the dinner table so I'm tryin' to keep him quiet." This seemed to satisfy Mama as she settled back into her eating routine.

Margaret looked at Allan and whispered, "Ask for the catsup."

Allan obeyed, "I want some catsup to put on this stuff."

I responded, "I'll get it." Then jumping up with my back to Mama, I dumped the rest of the unwanted food into the trash can.

I grabbed the catsup and a hand-full of napkins before returning to the table. Coming up behind Allan to hand off the catsup, my back to Mama, I mouthed to everyone, "One more round, that's all. Need more talkin'."

On cue, Margaret said, "I found some cactus on the hill."

Allan questioned, "What's cactus?"

"A plant with needles," answered Kirk.

Allan replied, "No it isn't. Plants don't have needles."

I motioned with my eyes and quietly formed the words, "OK, on three, scrape. One, two, three." Scraping sounds were barely audible.

Covering up any scraping sound Bill insisted, "This plant does." Looking at Margaret, he asked, "Where did you see it?"

"Over by the swing set on the hill. It's just a little one, hard to see. When I tried to pick it up, I got two needles in my finger, see? It's still red and one of the needles is still in my finger."

Disbelieving, Allan argued, "Is not. Let me see."

Butting into the conversation, I instructed barely audible, "Again, on three, pass. One, two, three." Slowly, yet carefully, napkins full of unwanted food were relayed to me for dumping.

Margaret stuck her right index finger toward Allan saying, "See, it's still red and swollen."

Allan asked, "Does it hurt?"

Responding, Margaret scrunched up her face, "Yeah it hurts. It hurts real bad. Don't ever touch a cactus plant. Don't 'cha remember last summer when I sat in some of that stuff and got needles in the back of my legs and hinny? Daddy had to help Mama pick 'em out. That really hurt."

Puzzled, Allan asked, "Then why did you sit in it?"

Margaret, irritated now, responded, "I didn't sit in it on purpose. Kat pushed me down and I fell on it. Just don't touch it."

Watching Mama cut a piece of steak, I jumped up announcing, "I need some more water to drink." Pushing the garbage can toward the sink with my foot, away from the den, I dumped my lap full of food-laden napkins into it while turning on the tap to fill my glass. Covering the evidence with empty corn and soup cans, I scooted the trashcan back into place before sitting down. Done!

"It's time for dessert," I announced.

Looking up from her place in the living room, Mama asked, "Did you eat everything on your plates?"

"I did, and it looks like everyone else did, too. What's for desserts?" I said answering her question and asking one of my own.

Ignoring Kat's question, Mama inquired, "Does anyone want seconds before I get the desserts?"

"No, Ma'am," everyone chimed in together.

"I'll be in there in a few minutes to get the desserts," Mama said.

"But what are we having for desserts?" Allan questioned.

"Carrot cake is in the refrigerator," Mama announced.

We all stared at each other with our noses turned up.

"Carrot cake? A cake made from carrots? That's what we're havin' for dessert?" I wanted to know.

"That's right. I think you'll like it. I had carrots left over from last night's supper and made a cake with them. As soon as I finish my meal, I'll be in to inspect your plates, and if you've eaten all your supper, I'll get each of you a piece of cake."

The five of us sat there dumfounded. We couldn't believe what we were hearing.

"We just got through dumpin' all of this yucky food into the garbage can and now we've got carrot cake for desserts. It's just not fair. All that work for nothin'. Who wants to eat a cake made of carrots? That's just not fair," I complained softly to my siblings.

"And besides I'm still very hungry. I was plannin' on the desserts fillin' me up," Bill whispered. "Now what are we gonna do?" he continued.

Meal times were interesting around our dinner table. We never knew what was for supper, but we always had a plan to get rid of the not-to-be-eaten food if it didn't meet our standards. Timing was everything, and we depended on each other as we collaborated each evening upon entering the dining room to face the unknown. As if we were one, we worked together in a silent conspiracy to arrive at the final goal – desserts.

But our elaborate plans were for naught that evening when Mama placed a slice of carrot cake in front of me and each of my siblings. Weary, hungry and discouraged, we stared in disbelief at the carrot cake set before us.

"Here we go again," I mumbled as Mama took her seat in the den.

WHICH IS WHICH?

Growing up as identical twins, we have had a lifetime of unique experiences, only a handful of which were told in this book. We knew at an early age that we were different since there were two of us and people marveled at our likeness. We always had each other to turn to, whether right or wrong, in the decisions that we made.

As the stories in this book unfolded, we trust you got a fix on our individual personalities. No matter how much we looked alike, our personalities were vastly different.

We invite you to go to our website, www.yalltwins. com, and vote as to "Which is Which?" Which twin listened to Mama and removed the jacket before the school-day pictures were made.

Also, find us on Facebook at facebook.com/kingtwins and on Twitter @TheKingTwins.

ABOUT THE AUTHORS

Katherine King graduated from The University of Mississippi in 1970 with a Bachelor of Arts in Secondary Education with an emphasis in mathematics. In 1971 she received a Master's of Education from The University of Mississippi with an emphasis in guidance and counseling and graduated with a Master's of Science in mathematics in 1986 from The University of Mississippi. During her teaching career, Katherine was twice named Star Teacher. In 2005, she received the Headwae Educator of the Year Award, recognizing her as the outstanding teacher at Northwest Community College. In 2008 Katherine was named the Lamplighter Educator of the Year from Northwest Community College. She is currently an

Instructor of Mathematics at the Oxford Campus of NWCC.

Margaret King graduated from The University of Mississippi in 1971 with a Bachelor of Arts in Education with an emphasis in secondary history. In 1973 she started her stint with the federal government as a courtroom clerk with US District Judge Orma R. Smith with the Northern District of Mississippi. After nine years she transitioned to Framers Home Administration/Rural Development. While working with Rural Development she twice received the highest honor given to a government employee – The Distinguished Service Award. She also received The Department of Army Commander's Award for Public Service, the highest civilian award given by the military. She is currently in semi-retirement.

Both authors find community service important. They belong to the Oxford Exchange Club where Margaret has served as president and ten years as secretary. Margaret is also a board member of The Exchange Club Family Center and former board member of the Oxford Boys and Girls Club. Both authors contribute to Back Pack for the Homeless, an organization that Margaret founded in the Oxford area. Katherine founded Santa Cause two years ago at NWCC whereby faculty and staff identity students and donate the gifts for their children for Christmas morning. They are both members of The United Methodist Church.

The King Twins, Katherine and Margaret, with Deuce
Photographs courtesy Emilie Bramlett